THEMES FOR TODAY   JAMES O'GARA, GENERAL EDITOR $2.95

o2

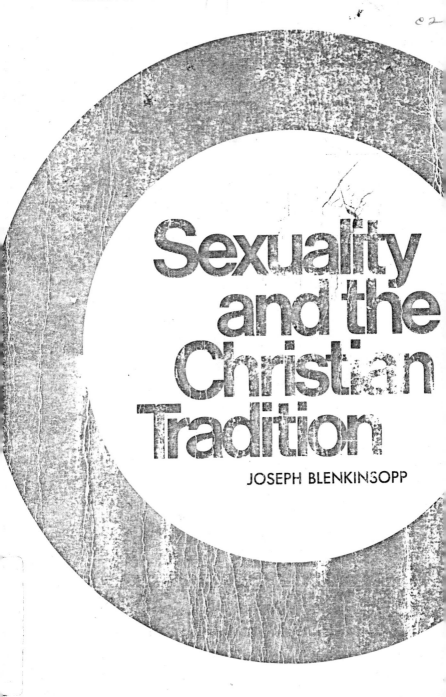

Sexuality and the Christian Tradition

JOSEPH BLENKINSOPP

Library of Congress Catalog Card Number: 79-93011

Pflaum Press
38 West Fifth Street
Dayton, Ohio   45402

JOSEPH
BLENKINSOPP

SEXUALITY AND THE CHRISTIAN TRADITION

PFLAUM PRESS, DAYTON, OHIO

1969

THEMES FOR TODAY
James O'Gara, General Editor

FOR IRENE

FOREWORD BY
GENERAL EDITOR

For years religion and religious institutions were thought of as relatively changeless. Indeed, for many this was precisely the great attraction of religion—it stood solid and rock-like, unchanging in the midst of a world very much in the process of change. Now those days have gone, probably forever. Today, change has become almost the normal condition. This change can be good or bad, obviously, and it is therefore more important than ever that we weigh and balance, that we exercise judgment wisely. It was for this reason that it seemed to the Editors of Pflaum Press and to me that a series of quality paperbacks would be helpful, a series specifically designed to take into account the fact of change. How do we visualize the goal of this series? Its purpose is simple, or at least is simply stated; books in the "Themes for Today" series will have one of two aims: to discuss the lasting and perennial in a contemporary fashion or to discuss the contemporary in a lasting fashion. If these goals are achieved, we will count the series a success.

JAMES O'GARA
Editor
Commonweal

ACKNOWLEDGMENTS

The author wishes to acknowledge the use of the following copyrighted material:

The Scripture quotations in this publication are from the Revised Standard Version of the Bible, copyrighted 1946 and 1952 by the Division of Christian Education of the National Council of the Churches of Christ in the U. S. A., and used by permission.

Selections from *Report to Greco* by Nikos Kazantzakis, copyright © 1965 by Simon & Schuster, Inc. Reprinted by permission of Simon & Schuster, Inc.

Excerpt from review of *Moralite sans Peche* by Paul Ricoeur in the Fall, 1955, issue of *Cross Currents*.

Selections from *New Theology No. 3* edited by Martin E. Marty and D. G. Peerman. Permission granted by Macmillan of New York.

Excerpt from *The Prophets* by Abraham J. Heschel, Harper & Row of New York, Publishers.

CONTENTS

Acknowledgments xi

Chapter One: Eros and the Christian 3

Chapter Two: The Single God 16

Chapter Three: Law or Love? 42

Chapter Four: Freedom 63

Chapter Five: The Silence of the Gospels 81

Chapter Six: Celebration 102

Index 123

SEXUALITY AND THE
CHRISTIAN TRADITION

EROS AND THE CHRISTIAN

It may seem an undertaking doomed from the outset to attempt a theological evaluation of the erotic in the context of the Judeo-Christian tradition and the biblical tradition in particular. The churches which have inherited and mediated this tradition have for so long seen their task primarily as one of issuing guidelines for conduct in sexual experience—defining what is not compatible with Christian love—that the logically antecedent task of interpreting sexual experience as such has passed by default to others who, more often than not, never seriously have considered that the tradition may have a positive contribution to make. Also, we are becoming more keenly aware of the lack of sound hermeneutical method in much of the work which has been done over the centuries. The result, at any rate, has been to create the impression that the tradition has little to tell us about the expansive possibilities of existence in general and of the man-woman relationship in particular, that it has no place for the celebration of *eros*. Christian experience, it is felt, is something generally hostile to erotic experience. And for too many Christians it is still unfortunately true that a deep separation exists between what they think of as "Christian" activities, especially church activities, and what is most deeply personal and affective in their lives.

Few would deny that in sexual ethics Christian moral theologians in general have been restrictive and deterrent. It may seem passé to speak of the predominance of legalism and

casuistry in Christian teaching on sexuality, but in fact neither term need have a pejorative connotation. It is surely legitimate to try to determine the minimal requirements for any act to be consistent in some way with a *Christian* experience of love. What is deplorable is not the determination of norms—though we might quarrel with the rationale behind the attempt—but the determination of norms apart from any statement of the maximal possibilities of erotic experience for the Christian.

At first sight it may seem hopeless to try to open lines of communication between what is generally called the Judeo-Christian tradition and contemporary experience, especially in the area of sexuality. For one thing, that tradition already has lost its hold, even if we think it is an important component in our culture. Many would regard it as simply a cultural residue from the past which owes its continued presence to the innate conservatism of religious thinking. Indications converge from many sides that we are moving into a new epoch, a new kind of consciousness, and this newness would be perhaps most visible in our sensitivity to the possibilities of sexual love. New openings are created at all levels with discussion panels on TV, the avant-garde theater and cinema, and, at a truly popular level, the whole morphology of sexual love in contemporary lyrics. This hardly can be interpreted as a fringe phenomenon, limited to the "psychodelic generation." Nor can it be limited to those with higher education, though the universities and colleges have played an important part in producing it. In view of the close collusion between organized Christianity and what is called "the American way of life," it may not be irrelevant to recall that, according to a recent Harris poll, thirty-three percent of Americans feel alienated from the mainstream of the national life.

Even more significant, however, is the fact that the most sensitive and perceptive of contemporary artists are generally unsympathetic to Christian ideas and teachings about sexuality even when they work, as they often do, with Christian symbols.

If, as Marshall McLuhan tells us, the artist is the antenna of the race, we should expect to find the new sexual consciousness in the artists of a previous generation. This is particularly true of those artists brought up in an actively Christian setting, which must have some relevance for present-day attitudes to the Christian tradition. Take the case of Ireland, where it is still possible to find a bishop who bans dancing in his diocese after midnight. It is no surprise to find that reaction against an oppressive attitude to sexuality emerges so clearly in voluntary exiles such as Joyce, O'Casey, Synge, and Edna O'Brien. In *Portrait of the Artist as a Young Man* Joyce has documented with unforgettable vividness how he had to "lose his soul" as a (Roman Catholic) Christian in order to save his soul as an artist. The ordeal by shame, the sexual guilt, the interminable exorcism of guilt in the confessional are only too familiar to the Roman Catholic reader. Dante's anger against those good Catholics who could not forgive Parnell's adultery is matched by that of Yeats against Dublin, the "blind, bitter town" which drove the cast of Synge's *Playboy of the Western World* off the stage for their supposed slur on Irish womanhood. From this point of view, the work of both Joyce and Yeats provides fascinating illustrations of both the prevalence of Christian imagery and symbols and the need to go beyond dominant Christian attitudes to human experience as a whole and sexual experience in particular.

Ireland is not, of course, an isolated example, only one where the issues become highly visible. It is also one in which the historical dimension can be more clearly delineated as a decisive factor. Never having been a part of the Roman Empire, its political and religious institutions took on a different form from that of the rest of Europe. The decisive influence in Ireland was Celtic monasticism with its mission to convert the world to its own idealistic and ascetical vision of Christianity, a mission which achieved, for a time at least, a large measure of success due to the fact that the episcopate was composed exclusively of monks. It would be no exaggeration to say that the object of these perfervid monks was to convert the world, and Ireland in particular, into a monastery. To this end a detailed rule of life was drawn up on the basis of the decalogue and the ritual laws of the Old Testament, with detailed sanctions imposed through the monastic penitential system and the practice of frequent confession.[1] With all due allowance for changed conditions, this was the system undergone by the young James Joyce (Stephen Daedalus) at Clongowes College.

The example of Ireland has been taken not because it is typical, which it is not, but because its relative isolation and religious homogeneity illustrate an important aspect of the issue under discussion. The celebrated trial of *Lady Chatterley's Lover* or the reaction of the Orthodox church to Kazantzakis' *The Last Temptation of Christ* and *The Greek Passion* would provide equally interesting case histories. The point is quite simply that the churches and their theologians have been very strong on moral evaluation and very weak on theological interpretation of sexual experience.

In view of all this, one question we want to ask in the following chapters is whether the Christian can accept his sexuality openly and without guilt or fear and whether he can integrate it into his total vision of faith. If this is not going to be possible, the inevitable consequence must be that more and more people will simply turn away from the Christian experience as a whole and look for answers elsewhere.

It may not be out of place to begin with a reflection on the vocabulary of love. It often has been noted that the word *eros* never occurs either in the New Testament or the Greek translations of the Old Testament. The only occurrence of the word in early Christian literature is in the letter of Ignatius of Antioch to the Roman Church, where he says that "my passionate love

---

[1] This is dealt with in greater detail by Albert Mirgeler, *Mutations of Western Christianity*, trans. Edward Quinn (New York: Herder and Herder, 1964), pp. 66-81.

(*eros*) has been crucified," which is reminiscent of what Paul says of the cross of Christ, by virtue of which "the world has been crucified to me and I to the world."[2] The obvious reason for the absence of *eros* from the Greek Bible would seem to be that the word connoted for the biblical writers, as it still does for us, passionate sexual love which goes beyond the bounds of rational and moral control. In the ancient Greek world, however, it did not primarily and necessarily have this meaning. In Greek philosophical writings *eros* refers to that impulse which leads man to go beyond himself, to become more than he is. For Empedocles, *eros* was the impulse towards union which he detected throughout the cosmos, something akin to the "radial energy" of Teilhard de Chardin. Plato immortalized it in the great discourse of the priestess Diotima in his *Symposium*. Here it signifies that mysterious energy which impels towards the possession of the good, the true, and the beautiful. It is the desire and pursuit of excellence and wholeness which includes within itself both rationality and passion.[3] Plato knew, of course, that many of his predecessors had described *eros* as a hostile, demonic, and tyrannical force, a kind of *hubris* which led man against all the power his reason could summon to his predestined fate. As is clear from the conversation preceding Diotima's *apologia*, Plato's understanding of how sexual love fits in with this all-inclusive desire is not without its ambiguities. The model of the perfect "erotic" relationship is not that between man and woman but between man and man or man and boy. Aristophanes' rather light-hearted presentation of the myth of the primitive hermaphrodite, put before his companions as an explanation of sexual differentiation, would imply that mutual sexual attraction between man and woman embodies something very close to what we would call alienation, facticity, or separation-anxiety. Yet, Plato's redefinition of *eros* at least

---

Ignatius, Rom. 7.2; Gal. 6:14.
See Thomas Gould, *Platonic Love* (New York: The Free Press, 1963), p. 32; also A. E. Taylor, *Plato: The Man and His Work*, 7th ed. (New York: Barnes & Noble, 1961), pp. 224-31, 305-9.

made it possible for others to understand sexual desire within the inclusive impulse toward self-transcendence.

While the ambiguities in the secular use of the word explain why it is not featured in the vocabulary of the Judeo-Christian tradition, they do not explain why other words are. Since both Greek translators and New Testament writers make frequent use of *agape,* a word which is practically unknown in the secular sphere, it might be supposed that *agape* stands for a different kind of love from *eros,* a love which is specifically Christian and removed from any sexual connotation. Thomas Aquinas expressed the difference as that between *benevolent love* (the kind God has shown to us) and *concupiscent love* (characteristic of fallen man), and in this form the distinction has become standard, at least in Roman Catholic teaching. The Lutheran theologian Anders Nygren, in his long-standing classic, *Agape and Eros,*[4] defined *eros* as acquisitive love (the Platonic type) and *agape* as the spontaneous love which God bestows on us through Christ and which is the measure of genuinely Christian love (what we might call the Pauline type). Both of these distinctions, which have much in common, *could* point toward a genuine understanding of sexuality in a Christian context. But they also could accentuate, especially in Nygren's presentation, the polarity between sexual love and Christian love and thus render an integrating solution more difficult. We hardly need demonstrate how prevalent among Christians of all denominations has been the view that the more perfect love is, the further it is removed from anything sexual.

If we turn to the Hebrew Bible we may find a more rewarding point of departure at the level of vocabulary. The Hebrew Scriptures use only one word for "love," whether of man for woman, man for man, man for God, or God for man. Dangerous as it is to draw rapid conclusions from such premises, we may take this to imply that for the Hebrew, *ahavah* (love) is

---

[4] Anders Nygren, *Agape and Eros,* trans. P. S. Watson (Philadelphia: Westminster Press, 1953).

always and everywhere the same in essence, a sharing in the universal movement which draws one being to another. And if this seems too large a claim at this stage, let us at least resist the temptation to equate *ahavah* with *eros,* and *hesed* (generally translated "steadfast love") with *agape. Hesed* is not a different kind of love from *ahavah*—certainly not divine as opposed to human love—but a *characteristic* of love which allows it, wherever it appears, to realize its full potential.

The importance of this observation is that it begins to reveal the possibility of integrating sexual love with the kind of self-transcending, self-immolating love to which the Scriptures witness. It also allows us to overcome the polarization of love into sexual and divine or agapitic, a polarization which has always been close to the surface throughout Christian history. The unfortunate consequence of this polarization is that it makes it difficult, if not impossible, to appreciate not just the ambiguities but also the possibilities of sexual experience. On the whole, passionate *eros* has been abandoned to the heretics and mystics (who were often also regarded as heretics), leaving the stage to the moral theologians—with well-known results.

The situation may be further clarified if we contrast *eros* with concupiscence in the sense in which this word has become current in Christian theology. The distinction of Aquinas, referred to a moment ago, would seem to be close to, if not identical with, the distinction between *agape* and *eros,* especially if we bear in mind the debt he owed to Augustine. No one, in fact, has been so influential as Augustine in giving currency and definition to the word "concupiscence"; and while it is true that he did not actually identify concupiscence with sexual desire, the devaluation of sex in his writings made the identification all too easy. Tillich has pointed out that the ambiguity surrounding this word has contributed greatly to the ambiguity toward sexuality in Christian attitudes. He goes on to propose that in order to clarify the issue, we must reaffirm that concupiscence has no necessary and certainly no exclusive relation to sexuality—otherwise it would be better to drop the word from our vocabulary. He defines concupiscence as "the unlimited desire to draw the whole of reality into one's self"; in which respect it is radically different from *eros,* which desires union with the other and not gratification obtained through the other. The concupiscent desire can take many forms, including the desire for limitless knowledge, as with Goethe's Faust, or for limitless power, as with Nero, or for limitless sexual gratification, as with Mozart's Don Juan.[5] The ambiguity in human sexuality is perhaps the most immediately obvious aspect of the condition of estrangement consequent on man's "fall" from the state of "dreaming innocence." Since man's condition is that of finite freedom, human sexuality can become one of the most powerful forms of that creative *eros* by which he goes out of himself and escapes from the hell of isolation and nonrecognition. But also it can manifest itself as a distorted and destructive form of the power of love and the exercise of freedom. The archetypal embodiment of this last is the figure of Don Juan. Tillich refers to the presentation of this figure by Kierkegaard, who describes the world of emptiness and despair in which Don Juan moves and the incapacity for creative love which drives him from one woman to another—an anticipation, perhaps, of Freud's discovery of the intimate relation between the libido and the "death wish."

Tillich's criticism of this emphasis on sex as concupiscence to the exclusion of its creative possibilities as a form of *eros* is certainly opportune. As against the Gnostics and Manicheans, the Christian view has always insisted that man is redeemed in the totality of his being. As he is born in the flesh, so is he also redeemed and glorified in the flesh. It is only when we accept this that we can go on to speak, with Ignatius, of the crucifixion of *eros.* His statement, and others like it, could easily be construed to mean that passionate love and love of the world are

---

[5]Paul Tillich. *Systematic Theology,* 3 vols. (Chicago: University of Chicago Press. 1951-63), 2:51-55.

obstacles to the Christian and have to be put out of the way. They *can* be obstacles, but so can the desire for money or knowledge or power. We should also note that these words come from a man on the way to the supreme sacrifice of martyrdom. Though still some way from martyrdom, Paul also wrote out of an acute consciousness of being at the end of an experience which began for him on the road to Damascus. All of his existence was caught up and transfigured in the light of this new experience. It is one thing to speak of *eros* transfigured or crucified at the end of such an experience and quite another to use this kind of language and make this kind of supposition at the beginning. To do so would not only be unreal, self-defeating, and self-destructive; it could also issue in doublethink and hypocrisy of a kind which has too often characterized Christian attitudes to sexuality—the kind castigated by D. H. Lawrence, for example. Erotic love, in the sense in which we now use the term, is real and remains real for the Christian. It cannot be wished away, written off or legislated out of existence. But it can be transformed.

Today, more than ever before, theological thinking and evaluation has to root itself in experience and sensitize itself to contemporary man's self-awareness and to the active environment which forms him. Christian doctrinal or moral teaching cannot be served up cold nor can the tradition be presented as providing answers to the probings of the contemporary mind. Appeals to maintain traditional formulations of doctrine and traditional modes of behavior more often than not fall on deaf ears, when they are heard at all. However difficult it may be to admit it, the tradition preserved in most of the churches today is simply nonviable. Despite demythologizing—perhaps in part because of it—answers are being given to questions which most people have stopped asking.

In this kind of situation, it could be argued that the basic problem is not one of authority or of church structures but of a genuine understanding of tradition; and the tragedy is that those churches which most emphasize authority are least aware of the ambiguities involved in appealing to tradition. Once we get beyond the idea of tradition as *merely* past, a corpus of doctrines and norms laid down once for all and delivered to the saints, we may find that it contains the seeds of its own rejuvenation if only we can recognize those seeds. But the price we have to pay is to start *at our end,* with our own experience and that of our contemporaries. What is still the "standard" approach to the tradition as the source of theological and moral teaching, according to which it must be presented unchanged to each successive generation, is contradicted at some critical points from within the tradition itself. This is too broad a subject to discuss at length, but two examples could be given. The prophets whose preaching has been preserved in the Old Testament obviously are deeply immersed in the sacred traditions of their people and refer constantly to exodus, covenant, the covenant law, and election. At the same time, however, they insist that in view of the new situation which faced Israel, the tradition must be radically reassessed. The Old Testament scholar Gerhard von Rad brings this out by contrasting the prophet with the mystic: ". . . even in their most sublime experiences the mystics always remained within the limits of the accepted dogmas of their own day, whereas the prophets, precisely in their inaugural visions, were led out to new vistas of belief."[6]

We might question whether mystics, in the Christian tradition at least, always remained within the bounds of orthodoxy, but there can be no doubt that the prophets as a whole challenged the orthodoxy and traditionalism of their contemporaries. Some of them, Jeremiah conspicuously, were clearly thought of by many as "heretics," as indeed was Jesus himself. Both Jeremiah and Jesus were concerned to make people *see* the new situation and evaluate the tradition accordingly. A similar kind of reassessment was called for by some of the wisdom teachers. It

---

[6]Gerhard von Rad, *Old Testament Theology,* trans. D. M. G. Stalker, 2 vols. (New York: Harper & Row, 1962-66), 2:62.

has always been a problem for scholars and readers of the Bible how books like Job and Ecclesiastes ever came to be regarded as Sacred Scripture. What we find, especially in the latter, is a conscious attempt to push traditional wisdom and the understanding of revealed faith toward the breaking point. And this is done by taking experience—not revelation—as the starting point and forcing the reader to look unflinchingly at it regardless of the consequences—especially with respect to ethical norms and the motivation for moral conduct. The lesson of both prophet and wisdom teacher is that tradition only comes into existence as an active force by being constantly challenged by experience.

Once we realize this, the consequences for the theme we are discussing will take on the greatest importance. For today, perhaps more than ever before, we are faced with a new situation. Consequently, the tradition, if it is to come into existence for us as an active force, must be faced with the challenge of this situation and resulting experience. Sociologists, anthropologists, theologians, situation ethicists, and others have spoken of this situation from their respective points of view. If, however, we wish to come closer to the center of awareness, we should turn to the creative artists, the "antennae of the race," or, as Kazantzakis put it, those "sensitive lips and fingertips which feel a tingling at a tempest's approach, as though they were being pricked by thousands of needles." The artists's approach more often than not will be one of indirection, but we should heed it nonetheless. To quote again from Kazantzakis:

We have been born in an important age full of kaleidoscopic experiments, adventures, and clashes, not only between the virtues and the vices, as formerly, but rather—and this is the most tragic of all— between the virtues themselves. The old, recognized virtues have begun to lose their authority; they are no longer able to fulfil the religious, moral, intellectual, and social demands of the contemporary soul. Man's soul seems to have grown bigger; it cannot fit any longer within the old molds. A pitiless civil war has broken out in the vitals of our age, has broken out, whether consciously or unconsciously, in the vitals of every man abreast of his times—a civil war between the old, formerly omnipotent myth which has vented its strength, yet which fights desperately to regulate our lives a while longer, and the new myth which is battling, still awkwardly and without organization, to govern our souls. That is why every living man is racked today by the dramatic fate of his times.[7]

If what Kazantzakis says about modern man breaking out of the old molds is true, it will be especially true in the understanding of sexual experience. This dictates the kind of question we want to ask in concert with the reader in what follows. Why is experience, especially sexual experience, so often removed from or imperfectly assimilated into the Christian vision? Is Yahweh, who is also the Christian God, a deity who continues to emasculate his children, as Freud supposed? Do Christ and *eros* oppose each other in the allegiance they lay upon us? Must we admit with Robert Gordis that ideally for the Christian "love and sex should be kept as far apart as possible, for the highest and purest form of love is that which does not eventuate in sexual fulfillment?"[8]

In order even to ask such questions as these, let alone answer them, we must have lived enough to have some experience of this civil war going on in the age we are living through. The collapse of ecclesiastical authority has left us in an open space where, if we are to continue to claim the title of Christian, we have to rediscover its meaning for ourselves apart from all we have been conditioned to think of as "religion." Yet, to rediscover it for ourselves does not mean that we have to work *by* ourselves. Even if, for the moment at least, we do not find a Christian community we can identify with, we are still working with others within the collective memory of the Christian community as a whole.

To close this chapter on a note of caution, it would be naive and nonproductive to attempt a Christian reinterpretation of sexual experience without being aware that we have to come to terms with the ambiguities, paradoxes, and tensions of being a

---

[7]Nikos Kazantzakis, *Report to Greco,* trans. P. A. Bien (New York: Simon & Schuster, 1965), Bantam Books, 1966, p. 434.

[8]Robert Gordis, "Re-judaizing Christianity," *The Center Magazine,* September, 1968, p. 13.

Christian in the world. There is, in short, no easy way past the "mourning as though not mourning, rejoicing as though not rejoicing" of Paul. There is no more an easy way of understanding the Christian reality than there is of living it. We cannot absolutize the received wisdom or the traditional symbols of Christian theology, but neither can we absolutize our own experience or that of our contemporaries. Whether we are aware of it or not (and if not, so much the worse for us), our past is present to us and weighs upon us, determining in sometimes hidden ways the mind-set we bring to the solution of our most personal problems. Progress will be conditional on dissolving a false understanding of our past, as in genuine therapy, and also on allowing the Christian past to address a prophetic challenge to our present self-understanding. In the following chapters I would like to contribute to this task by bringing to the surface some ambiguities in "traditional" Christian attitudes to sexual experience and by looking at some aspects of the Judeo-Christian tradition. In this way we may find help in coming to terms with and interpreting our continuing experience.

THE SINGLE GOD

Now that the perceptive Christian has broken away (or simply turned away) from the deterrent and nomistic approach to sexuality inculcated by "church authority," what is there for him to hang onto or where can he turn for help? Around us is a landscape littered with unpersuasive dogmas, broken symbols, and the charred fragments of tradition. We still seem to need some framework or context within which to understand erotic experience and integrate it into a viable coming to terms with ourselves. Even religious language and symbolism still seem to be necessary to express erotic meaning; not just in the moment of hurt or ecstasy but in the long times between. To judge by the idiom in which popular love-lyrics are still being composed (adoration, rapt ecstasy, et cetera), "philosophies" will not suffice and sexual symbols come at us from every direction. Yet, the fact remains that with the dissolution of culture-Christianity, it is now up to the individual to find some integrative framework for understanding, articulating, and living out—or only just coping with—the erotic. As is well known, this need was met in antiquity by myths which served the purpose of psychological and social integration. It is often being said that the mass media have created comparable myths for us today. Harvey Cox, for example, maintains that Miss America "stands in a long line of queens going back to Isis, Ceres and Aphrodite,"[1] but such a statement seems to confuse myth with an archetypal figure; and we may also ask how anything so nonparticipatory, voyeurist,

---

[1] Harvey Cox, *The Secular City* (New York: Macmillan paperback, 1965), p. 194.

16

and artificial can be compared seriously with the functional and operative figures of which he speaks.

We can hardly doubt that, in practice, widely accepted Christian approaches to sexual experience have contributed to isolating and depersonalizing *eros* and have provoked into existence "philosophies" of sex which have continued the same process from different angles. In other words, some powerful influences at work within mainstream church-Christianity have tended toward the separation of "love" and "sex," thereby becoming powerful factors in the disintegration of the sexual, which is what we have to live with today. By helping to build up a reservoir of fear and guilt vis-à-vis sexual experience, historical Christianity, in particular, has contributed to what D. H. Lawrence called "sex in the head"—a split between mind and body and a consequent cerebralization of sex. This explains a good part of our difficulty in coming to grips with the lifelong task of humanizing and integrating the erotic into the spiritual environment in which Christians live today.

Given this situation, we would like to suggest not a new religious approach, much less a philosophy (we have had too many of these), but a reexamination of the Judeo-Christian tradition in its understanding of sex in the life of the individual and of society. The method will be more that of picking up hints and working by way of indirection since, despite a long and illustrious list of publishers' titles, there is no such thing as a biblical or Christian theology of sexuality. Another point which is so obvious that it hardly needs to be mentioned is that Judaism and Christianity betray very considerable differences in their understanding of sexuality, despite the fact that they have a common starting point. We shall have to pay attention both to these differences and to competing ways of understanding sexuality within each tradition. But, for the moment, our starting point has to be the Jewish Scriptures which early Christianity took over and renamed the Old Testament. What we find in this vast and confusing collection is, in the first place, what

Merleau-Ponty called "the linguistic debris of the past." If any of this is to speak to us in our different situation today we have to make it speak by asking questions of it and allowing it in its turn to question us. This implies that we must first understand the "word-event" which called it into existence, the situation in which it arose and to which it spoke, and the understanding of existence which it embodies.[2] As far as the erotic is concerned, this has to take in an understanding of the mythical world in the midst of which these writings came into existence. Only in this way will we be able to give an account of what happened when the world of myth impinged upon and interpenetrated the experience and faith of Israel. The justification is that the results of this encounter are still with us as, hopefully, we shall see.

Ancient myths which speak of the not so secret lives and loves of gods and goddesses can no longer be considered purely the product of fantasy, what Bergson called *"la fonction fabulatrice."* For the ancients, myth was the only means at hand for attempting some kind of all-inclusive interpretation of existence. It was, in other words, the only way open to them of challenging the world to render some meaning, of imposing order on chaos and at the same time of living out the discovered meaning. To take an obvious example, the myths of dying and rising gods not only gave expression to an intuition about life and death, they were also functional. The community, by acting out the myth, believed it possible to promote its essential economic interests based on the fertility of the womenfolk, the herds, and the fields. Even after the dawn of philosophical reason, myth continued to be used, if in a more detached and sophisticated way, to express what could not be put into discursive language. Aristotle considered it legitimate to "philosophize by means of myth"; and Plato did not scruple to make use of the symbolic language of myth, even though he expelled the *mythologoi* from his utopian

---

[2]The term "word-event" and its general connotation derive from Gerhard Ebeling, especially his *Word and Faith* (Philadelphia: Fortress Press, 1963).

state. The creation of the world is expressed in mythical terms in *Timaeus*; the myth of Er at the end of the *Republic* communicates in a way impossible to rational discourse what Plato felt about the destiny of the human soul; and the eros-myth of Aristophanes in the *Symposium* speaks of the origin and nature of sexual differentiation.

In different ways both Tillich and Jung have indicated the need of integrative symbols corresponding functionally to the collective representations of the ancients. We cannot say yet whether this kind of integration is still open to us in the fast-moving technological epoch of today, but some integration surely is necessary. Integrative systems have been on the market for some time: the visceral mysticism of the D. H. Lawrence type, the "good orgasm" of Henry Miller and Norman Mailer, the "sex as healthy sport" philosophy of Alex Comfort, the "philosophy" of Hugh Hefner, and so on. If our aim is wholeness, that is, integration of the erotic into personhood as a whole, we shall evaluate the above systems as they contribute to personalizing and humanizing human sexuality. All of them point to the necessity of some integrating view and the difficulty of achieving it. In their own way, so do some recent papal encyclicals, conspicuously *Humanae Vitae*. However, let us begin our probing not with the relation between sexuality and integrating systems, nor even with the relation between sexuality and religion in general, but with one precise phenomenon in the history of religions which will lead on to something of great importance in the Judeo-Christian tradition. This phenomenon, discoverable at all points of ancient mythical thinking, is the attribution of sexuality to the divine persons who are the dramatis personae of the myths.

At first glance, this may seem so obvious as not to be worth talking about. Yet, if we recall that myths are essentially paradigmatic and functional, it will be obvious that this must have something to do with articulating and perhaps also authenticating the role of the sexual in the society which accepts and lives by the myth. The god and his consort provide the archetype for the human sexual partners. The representation of creation as procreation (as in ancient Greece, Egypt, and Mesopotomia) speaks symbolically of the creative place of sex and fertility in an agrarian society. But the myth is more than a paradigmatic story. To *mythos*, the spoken word, corresponds *dromenon*, the action or drama. The spoken word, the libretto, is ancillary to the ritual action or mime by which the archetypal event is brought into the present and experienced anew. The relation between myth (understood in this sense) and ritual or cult is expressed as follows by the Norwegian Old Testament scholar Sigmund Mowinckel:

> The cult is not only by its origin, but in all places and at all times, drama. The cult is sacred art. But at the same time it is sacred reality, not merely an acted drama or a play, but a real drama and one that manifests reality, a drama which realizes the dramatic event with real power, a reality from which real forces emanate, in other words it is a sacrament. The cult of primitive man is this and nothing else. . . . The basic idea is this: that through the dramatic, 'symbolic' presentation, realization and reanimation of the particular event, this event is actually and really repeated; it repeats itself, happens all over again and exercises afresh the same mighty, redemptive effect that it exercized for our salvation on the first occasion at the dawn of time or in the far distant past.[3]

An example of this functional aspect of mythical thinking would be the marriage between the king and a temple prostitute which took place at the end of the Babylonian New Year festival or the ritual orgy as practiced in Canaan. What we have in both cases is an acting out of the marriage between the male heaven and the female earth. Despite the condemnation of such practices in the Hebrew laws and prophets, it is entirely possible to view them within the context of meaning outlined by Mowinckel and therefore as dictated by a high moral seriousness. They were acts concerned with the good of the community as a whole and

[3]S. Mowinckel, *Psalmenstudien*, Vol 2, p. 21. Quoted in Hans-Joachim Kraus, *Worship in Israel*, trans. G. Buswell (Richmond, Va.: John Knox Press, 1966), p. 5.

among the most sacred in which the community participated. If all we found in the Old Testament was condemnation of such practices, we would be justified in asking by what right the Hebrews passed judgement on their predecessors. After all, the Canaanites were never given a chance to state their own side of the case and reply to their accusers.

Less obvious is the myth's attempt to articulate and, at the same time, cope with the demonic and disruptive in human sexuality. No man, says one of the wisdom writers, can carry fire in his bosom without being burned, and the sages and poets of all ages have borne him out—

> *Nulla unda tam profunda*
> *Quam vis amoris furibunda . . . .*

This theme, embodied for the Greeks in the figure of Dionysus, who has passed into modern currency especially under the influence of Nietzsche, is present only cryptically in the myths with which the Hebrews were familiar. To the chaos out of which the order of creation emerges corresponds the chaotic in sexuality. In the Babylonian creation-myth, read on the fourth day of the week-long New Year festival, the world is created out of the dismembered body of Tiamat, a female monster who is also the consort of the high god Apsu. Tiamat represents the primeval sea, the watery deep with its uncontrollable currents which threatens at all times to swamp the narrow beachhead of civilization won by the technique of irrigation in the Euphrates basin. To Tiamat corresponds the *tehom* or "deep" of the creation recital in the first chapter of Genesis (*tehom* is evidently associated with Tiamat). It will not escape us that for both the historian of religions and the psychoanalyst, water is *the* sexual symbol. Therefore, we may find here a veiled allusion to the limitless, uncontrollable, and disruptive element in human sexuality which is, so to speak, built into the natural order and which yet must be contained.

Those who, like the present writer, have never participated in a sexual orgy, will have to depend on the fallible evidence of hearsay, paperbacks, or the cinema in surmising that they are, as a general rule, devoid of any specific religious character. The historian of religions will tell us that in antiquity the orgy was a ritual and religious act signifying a return to the point at which creation emerged from chaos. At the same time it was a means of breaking down barriers so that the primal creative energy could flow unhindered through the community. And precisely because it was a religious act, a sacred institution restricted to certain crucial transitional occasions in the calendar, it also represented an attempt to *contain* the demonic inseparable from the creative in sexuality. We could see it, perhaps, as corresponding on the psychological level to the need of integrating the shadow, a need which appears to be not only individual but social. The modern parallel to the sacred orgy of antiquity would not be, we may suspect, of the *Dolce Vita* variety. We should rather look for it in the carnival as it occurs, sometimes in spectacular fashion, in Latin countries. Attempts by the Christian church to suppress this practice have been as persevering and as unsuccessful (if not more so) than the attempts of the Hebrew legislators and prophets to get rid of the Canaanite orgy.

The polarity between the creative and destructive in human sexuality also comes to expression in the archetypal figure of the goddess who seduces and destroys. Something like this appears in the Indian goddess Kali, whom several texts describe as gentle and affectionate but who nevertheless often is represented in sculpture wearing a necklace of human skulls dripping with blood.[4] Coming closer to the culture with which the early Hebrews were familiar, we find in the Gilgamesh epic, popular throughout the ancient Near East, two classical cases of this kind of seduction. The hero's friend, Enkiddu, accepts the advances of a footloose goddess, and they make love for the space of an entire week. Later, however, he discovers that the animal world has turned away from him, and shortly afterward he dies

---

[4] M. Eliade, *Patterns in Comparative Religion* (New York: Meridian Books, n.d.), pp. 418ff.

of a mysterious ailment.[5] Gilgamesh himself is less impetuous. Accosted by Ishtar, goddess of passionate love (the counterpart of the Greek Aphrodite), he turns away her advances by sarcastically reminding her of her many previous affairs. In the fragmentary tale of the legendary hero Aqhat, discovered among the tablets at Ugarit (Ras Shamra) in Syria, the Canaanite goddess Anath tries to wheedle the hero's bow from him and when he refuses has him destroyed. Elsewhere she is described as not only passionate but bloodthirsty. In the fertility myth it is she who dismembers Mot the god of the grain. She wades up to her thighs in the blood of her enemies and even threatens El, the supreme god of the pantheon, if he refuses to comply with her wishes:

> I shall make thy gray hairs run with blood,
> The gray hairs of thy beard with gore![6]

In all of these cases, we find projected into the timeless world of myth an insight into that element of human sexuality which is less personal and amenable to control.

A further case of ambivalence ought to be noted. It is certainly true in some cases, and may be true in general, that the divine sexual partners (Thammuz and Ishtar, Isis and Osiris, Anath and Baal, et cetera) stand for a primitive androgynous being.[7] Granted this, we may find in the archetypal, mythical world an intuition of unity behind sexual differentiation and the sex act as the means of returning to a primordial unity. I suppose it might be argued that both the study of the evolutionary development of sexual differentiation and human biology provide some explanation and support of this intuition; but what is important is to grasp it in terms of its own meaningful inten-

---

[5] E. A. Speiser, *Genesis* (The Anchor Bible) (New York: Doubleday, 1964), pp. 26ff., suggests an association between this episode and the temptation scene in Genesis 3.

[6] C. H. Gordon, *Ugaritic Literature* (Ventnor, N. J.: Ventnor, 1947), pp. 17ff.

[7] Eliade, *Patterns in Comparative Religion*, pp. 420-22.

tionality. What seems to come to expression here is one aspect of a movement to integrate man's whole psychic and social life with the unchanging processes of a divine world of nature. In the Platonic myth of the original hermaphrodite, on the contrary, the main point seems to be to explain the mutual attraction of the sexes as an aspect of what we might call alienation. It is in this more self-conscious form that the myth has exerted such an influence, generally not good, on Christian thinking. No doubt it also lies behind the idea, often expressed in Romantic poets like Wordsworth and Shelley, that the partners in sexual intercourse are, in some ill-defined way, dissolved into a cosmic process—"the rivers mingle with the ocean, why not I with thee?"

What we find, at any rate, in the myths of antiquity, and of Semitic antiquity in particular, are various ways of expressing the transpersonal in human sexuality, of consecrating and reactivating it. This is the background against which we have to view the biblical tradition.

Studied within this environment, the most remarkable thing about the Jewish Scriptures is that the god of whom they speak is celibate. Not only does he not have a goddess at his side as is elsewhere universally the case, there is not even a word for "goddess" in Hebrew. That popular religious sentiment, deeply influenced by the Canaanite environment, insisted on providing him with a consort is clear, of course, from the record. We read, for example, that Maacah set up an image of the fertility goddess, Asherah, in Jerusalem (1 Kings 15:13), though the writer makes it quite clear that this was one of the main reasons for her deposition from the influential position of queen-mother. The goddess Asherah, mentioned more than forty times in the Old Testament, was almost certainly thought of by many of those who remained impervious to prophetic preaching as the wife of Yahweh. In the Ras Shamra texts she is the consort of El, and we know that from an early period attempts were made to identify Yahweh with the supreme god of the Canaanite pantheon (there are scholars who think his original title was Yahweh-El).

In the fifth century before Christ, we find the Jewish colonists at Elephantine in Upper Egypt worshiping Yahweh side by side with Anath, consort of Baal, to some of whose less amiable characteristics we referred earlier. Both Asherah and Anath were fertility goddesses, and their roles tended to get confused. That both exercised great fascination on the Hebrews can be seen from the legislation and the history. Jeremiah follows closely on Hosea his mentor in denouncing this addiction to the fertility cult, and the frequent occurrence in both prophets of the verb *zanah*—referring to sexual irregularity and apostasy—provides a good indication of the allure of the local shrines serviced by cultic prostitutes. Jeremiah speaks of his fellow countrymen worshiping "the queen of heaven" (Jer. 7:18; 44:17); and Ezekiel, in the course of his guided tour of the Jerusalem temple, was shown the statue of a fertility goddess north of the main gate (Ezek. 8:3).

These and many more indications of syncretism, however, do not alter the fact that Yahweh comes before us in the earliest sources and in prophetic preaching as without spouse and without offspring. In the context of the environment and of religious practice at that time, this is a fact so extraordinary that it deserves closer attention and may prove to be very relevant for the theme we are investigating.

To begin at the most obvious point: one consequence of the celibacy of the Hebrew god is that for Israel the prototypal sexual partnership is not divine but human. This at once suggests a radical departure from the world of mythical meanings and, in particular, a positive demythologizing and desacralizing of sexuality. The function of human sexuality in society is no longer derived from mythical archetypes but from reflection on experience. So many dogmatic statements have been hung on the story of the Man and the Woman in the garden (Gen. 2-3) that this may not be immediately obvious, apart from the difficulty that the writer has obviously conscripted myths to serve his purpose. Yet, it is not difficult to show that this apparently artless story comes from a milieu, that of the court during the early monarchy, which was under the influence of wisdom teachers and sufficiently detached from myth to bring off this kind of masterpiece. Comparison with the history of the succession to David's throne, leading dramatically to the accession of Solomon (2 Sam. 11–1 Kings 2), will reveal both clear traces of wisdom influence and the presence of the same themes as are found in the first episode of the Yahwist's work. It will also show how myth has been taken out of its original thought-context and employed as a means of giving universal validity to reflection arising out of a particular area of experience. Hence, the story of the Man and the Woman should be read neither as history nor as myth but as a dramatic paradigm born of experience, perhaps the finest and the most sophisticated piece of wisdom writing in the Old Testament.[8]

The nearest the Old Testament comes to the widespread myth of cosmogonic eros is the obscure fragment about divine beings ("the sons of God") mating with human women ("the daughters of men") and bringing forth a race of promiscuous titans (Gen. 6:1–4). It is interesting that this passage rather than the story of "Adam" features here and there in Jewish and early Christian tradition as the original sin story. It is equally interesting that the story of "Adam," which was to become of such overwhelming importance, is never again mentioned in the Jewish Scriptures. But even in Genesis 6:1–4, which is the most frankly mythological piece of literary debris that we find in the Old Testament, there is no myth in the real sense of that word. Strictly speaking it is only a mythical motif which came in useful at that point to express a moral judgment on the pre-Israelite inhabitants of the land on account of whose sexual promiscuity (so the author thought) God decided to open the floodgates of judgment. Finally, there may be a veiled warning in both passages against marriage with non-Israelite women,

---

[8] I have dealt with this at greater length in the *Supplement to Vetus Testamentum* 15 (1966): 44-57 and in *A Sketchbook of Biblical Theology* (New York: Herder and Herder, 1968), pp. 50-56.

since experience has shown that such marriages often had disastrous effects.

What we find, then, in the Jewish Scripture is a radical and conscious break with the world of myth insofar as it provided a context for speaking about the role of the sexual in society. Female chaos (Tiamat) is depersonalized and desexed and becomes the watery deep (*tehom*). The theme of the goddess who seduces and destroys is restated in terms of human experience— the old theme of the *femme fatale* which occurs with some regularity in the Hebrew and Jewish wisdom writers.[9] Sexual partnership is authenticated with reference to a paradigmatic couple—the Man and the Woman—and, strangely enough, in a way which does not reflect the dominative view of marriage prevalent in Hebrew society as elsewhere in Semitic antiquity. Sexual differentiation is not explained with reference to a divine couple or a bisexual deity; it derives from a creative word of God by which mankind (*adam*) exists as male and female (Gen. 1:27). Despite the statement in Gen. 5:3 about Adam becoming the father of Seth "in his own likeness, after his image," it is impossible to suppose that the image of God refers to the ability to (pro)create. Yahweh is nowhere represented as a procreative deity like El and Zeus. It would refer more naturally to the belief that man is the representative of God in exercising dominion over the creative world and, as such, is placed just a little below God (Ps. 8:5).

We can hardly exaggerate the importance of this radical departure from an age-old pattern of thinking, no matter how imperfectly it was carried through. For what is expressed in these ancient myths is an existence determined and closed in on itself, bound by laws to which even the gods are subject. Man can never be free of the demonic forces which hedge him in. He can, at the most, placate them, attempt to contain them, but he remains at the final count at the mercy of the impersonal forces

---

[9] Especially in the Yahwist and wisdom teachers. See below pp. 113-114.

within himself and the dark, circumambient elements which threaten him from outside. By accepting covenant with Yahweh the single god, Hebrew man certainly created some new problems for himself, but he also made it possible to achieve freedom from the impersonal, to escape from the closed circle and move out into a genuinely personal life-project. Here we touch a crucial point in the tradition which we have inherited. For Greek thought at all levels, even that of the great tragedians (especially in *Antigone*), *eros* is a dark force, a kind of *hubris* which leads man where he would not go, a mighty demon against which it is useless to struggle. If we turn to the early historical narratives in the Old Testament, especially to that which begins with the adultery of David in which the role of the sexual is frankly portrayed, it is clear throughout that it is not beyond man's power of control. The same emerges in the story of the first couple, and Yahweh tells Cain that though the demon is couching at the door of his tent, he can overcome it (Gen. 4:7). To take a final example, it is no surprise that the story of Joseph and Potiphar's wife recurs so often in Jewish tradition as an example of triumph over sexual temptation. It is certainly difficult for us today to realize what a radical departure this was from the general trend of thinking at that time.

We spoke a moment ago of the myth of divine androgyny, which clearly in some cases and implicitly in others lies behind the divine sexual partners of antiquity. In view of the functionality of this kind of representation, the celibacy of Yahweh would imply the rejection of any kind of sexual mysticism aimed at restoring a lost unity through unrestrained sexuality, a return to a kind of fetal sentience. Indian erotic mysticism, something of which can now be sampled by a trip to the nearest drugstore, aimed at perfecting man by taking him through the barrier of sexual differentiation to a unity of being which lay beyond.[10] Something of the same idea seems to be present in the ancient practice of the sexes exchanging clothing during

---

[10]Eliade, *Patterns in Comparative Religion*, p. 421.

orgiastic rites. Judging by the prohibition of transvestism in Hebrew legislation (Deut. 22:5) this was widely practiced in Canaan, and later Greek authors tell us that it was a common feature of the worship of Ishtar, goddess of love. Whether this has any relevance for the noncultic practice of transvestism today is a question which we leave to the clinical psychologist. This and other forms of what Aldous Huxley called "downward self-transcendence" were resisted by the prophets as hostile to the covenant and the relational way of thinking which stemmed from it.

That some rabbis indulged in rather extravagant speculations about an androgynous Adam may well be due to the allure of Platonic thinking. It seems clear, at all events, that the Bible knows nothing of either divine or human androgyny and, therefore, testifies firmly to individuality and mutuality in erotic experience. The abolition of sexual mysticism cost dearly; yet, it was, and continues to be, a necessary step towards the achievement of freedom for an existence which is genuinely personal and relational. In the scriptural area of meaning, *man exists as response* both to the call of being and the word which is addressed to him by the other. Relational existence means a continual calling into being of the other as I, in my turn, am continually called into being by him. This opens the way to overcoming the dichotomizing of sex as either demonic or institutionalized (in marriage) and to understanding it in the categories of communication, language, address, and response. These are general statements, the implications of which we shall have to pursue at a later point.

We hardly need say how difficult it has been throughout the Jewish and Christians traditions to maintain a genuine individuality and mutuality in the understanding of the erotic. It has, on the whole, been less difficult in the former since Judaism has been less open, precisely because of the nature of its claims, to the contamination of foreign influences. As far as the Christian tradition is concerned, pressure has come from both sides of a delicate and thin line. But since the various forms of sexual mysticism were rapidly banished to the heretical fringes by a church dominated by the celibate ideal, much more pressure and influence have been exerted from the side of antisexual mysticism. Right from the early days, there has been a tendency to separate agapitic and erotic love and to depreciate the latter in favor of the former. To take one important and crucial example: Gnostic speculations of the kind contained in the so-called Gospel of Thomas discovered less than a quarter of a century ago in Egypt. This collection of sayings attributed to Jesus, which comes apparently from the fourth century, also speaks of the dissolution of sexual differentiation as a necessary step towards perfection. This perfect state will come only when "you make the man (with) the woman a single one, in order that the man is not man and the woman is not woman."[11] The woman is not worthy of life until she becomes male through the virginal spirit. Of Miriam (probably Mary Magdalene rather than Mary, the Mother of Jesus) Jesus says:

Lo, I will draw her
So that I will make her a man
So that she too may become a living spirit
Which is like you men;
For every woman who makes herself a man
Will enter into the kingdom of heaven.[12]

This, of course, comes from a Gnostic Christian group which was outside the ecclesiastical mainstream and which imposed its own interpretation on biblical texts. Gnostic groups like the Naassenes interpreted Genesis 1:27 as the creation of an androgynous being which remains the ideal. They also took the saying of Jesus against lust in Matthew 5:27-30 as an absolute prohibition of intercourse. Yet, in questions of attitudes, the line

---

[11] R. M. Grant and D. N. Freedman, *The Secret Sayings of Jesus* (New York: Doubleday, 1960), p. 143.
[12] *Ibid*, p. 197.

between what is and is not orthodox is not always easy to draw. Once Christianity had broken out of its Jewish chrysalis and had begun to make its way in the Greek-speaking world beyond Palestine, once it had begun to be accepted, practiced, and defended by philosophers under the allure of Platonic thought, this kind of attitude easily took hold. Given this situation, some statements in the Christian Scriptures could easily be interpreted as supporting this attitude. For example, what Paul says (Gal. 3:28) about there being neither male nor female in Christ Jesus obviously seemed to point in the same direction, though it is extremely doubtful whether Paul himself had anything like this in mind.[13] It is at least clear that the dichotomy between love and sexuality and the view of sexual differentiation as basically a form of alienation were not confined to groups outside the mainstream.

Let us return for the moment to our point of departure in the celibacy of the Hebrew (and therefore Christian) God. One further consequence ought to be mentioned, though it can be expressed only tentatively and by way of indirection. The absence of a consort alongside Yahweh has often been thought to have something to do with an authoritarian and nomistic attitude toward sexual conduct, which is noticeable in the tradition and has been fastened onto by the moral theologians. While it is more often the mother who "emasculates" the son, there is a sense in which the father is the rival of the son on the way to manhood. Whatever we may think of his thesis as a whole, in *Totem and Taboo* and *Moses and Monotheism*, Freud at least

---

[13] Paul's misogynism has been exaggerated greatly, and, of course, there is no evidence for Gnostic tendencies in his thinking. Those who interpret this text as evidencing either misogyny or Gnostic influence have generally overlooked the close parallelism with the three fold blessing in the Jewish morning prayers: "blessed art thou Lord our God who hast not made me a Gentile . . . a slave . . . a woman." Nor can this latter be used to charge Judaism with antifeminism. Man is more blessed than woman simply because by nature he can fulfil more of the stipulations of the Torah than a woman.

pointed out some ambiguities involved in attributing fatherhood to God. His hypothesis of an earlier Yahweh-cult based on the religious reforms of Ikhnaton, suppressed after the murder of Moses by his followers and supplanted by the worship of the demonic Yahweh of Kadesh, probably will not win many adherents in the scholarly world today. Likewise, his characterization of Yahweh of Kadesh as "an uncanny, bloodthirsty demon who walks by night and shuns the light of day" may well be an evident exaggeration. At the same time, it is impossible to deny that there is a strong element of the demonic in the character of the Old Testament God, at least in the earlier period. He is often angry and passionate, is not above tempting people like David and Ahab to pursue ruinous courses, and is capable of producing precisely engineered earthquakes to swallow up unwitting offenders. Perhaps we also may find here and there old mythological themes imperfectly assimilated to Hebrew faith, such as that of the god's jealousy of man's happiness and freedom (". . . lest he put forth his hand and take also of the tree of life!"). Hypothetical as this is, surely we may ask whether there is not a sense in which, sooner or later, the son does not have to challenge the father, whether man may not challenge the omnipotent and omnipresent father-figure not only in order to be free but also to know the father's true face.

It is surely this deep and, to the conventional religious man, shocking insight which led to the inclusion of the Book of Job in sacred Scripture. Not only in Job but also in the Psalms and the prophets and elsewhere do we find men at the breaking point who in their manhood turn their faces and question the god who pursues them.

It would not be difficult to show how this fierce father has passed over into the subconscious of very many Christians. After hearing in bible class of the Old Testament God, Yahweh, the "ravenous beast of the celestial jungle," the young Kazantzakis went off by himself and prayed, "Father, we do not want you to

eat us!" Nor was he far removed from the mind of Job when he said that "the true man is he who resists, struggles and is not afraid, in time of great need, to say no, even to God."[14] According to Freud, the religious neurosis began historically with the killing and eating of the father—the dominant male of the primitive horde—and the guilt induced by this act of murder and cannibalism. It continues to revolve around the fear of and longing for the father. The revulsion against incest derives from the feared will of the father, and the practice of circumcision is a symbolic substitute for castration carried out by the father on his sons. Granted the fragility of these theses (Freud was always a little cavalier in the matter of historical research), we still ought to give due attention to this demonic element before passing on to speak of a purification of the image throughout the history of the tradition. We should also note how it bred an inevitable reaction in the continuous attempt to right the balance by reasserting the female element—paradoxically since, as we have seen, the demonic is so often personified as female in the mythical world from which the Hebrews broke away. Right down to the dawn of Judaism in the exilic age, popular religion resisted the celibacy of its god, and the victory of prophetic preaching over the orgiastic and ecstatic cults was never complete and often a downright failure. In early Judaism we may perhaps detect a more refined version of the same tendency in the hypostasizing of wisdom (equated with the Torah), similar to the personification of the female Spirit in the Christian East and some exaggerated forms of devotion to the Virgin Mary. All of this emphasizes the difficulty of freeing thought from divine archetypes and of effectively desacralizing and demythologizing sexuality. And we would be very naive to suppose that we have yet succeeded in doing this.

The humanization of sexuality is an essential aspect, perhaps

---

[14] Nikos Kazantzakis, *Report to Greco,* trans. P. A. Bien (New York: Simon & Schuster, 1965), Bantam Books, 1966, p. 72.

the essential aspect, of growth towards genuine personhood. It requires freedom from domination by the impersonal and demonic elements inherited from the past. We have seen how in antiquity mythological monsters embodied these negative, impersonal, and demonic aspects of psychic and societal experience. Babylonian Chaos, the female monster, becomes, so to speak, the raw material of the created world; but she is also the dark spouse of the high god Apsu. The possibility of containing Chaos had to be reaffirmed annually in the *akitu,* the New Year Festival. The inability of Hebrew faith to take these projections seriously, together with the persistent need to project, resulted in an unresolved tension in the way Yahweh was thought of. Given this state of things, we may say that the emergence of the figure of Satan was a theological necessity. That is to say, Satan only appears when it becomes impossible to project the "satanic" onto Yahweh. Thus, an historian of the early monarchy describes a pestilence during the reign of David and attributes the evil directly to Yahweh (2 Sam. 24:1) while the Chronicler, writing half a millennium later, makes Satan (the Adversary) responsible (1 Chron. 21:1). It is true that there is nothing sexual about this personification of the demonic at its first appearance.[15] Yet, it was inevitable that Satan should sooner or later have been identified with the tempting Serpent of the Yahwist's origins-story, as he is explicitly in the Wisdom of Solomon (2:24) and in the Book of Revelation (12:9). The ascription of sexual temptation and disaster to Satan or one of his minions (Asmodeus in the rather fantastic tale of Tobit) began early, was greatly promoted by the monks and hermits (witness the life of Saint Anthony), reached fantastic proportions in the long epidemic of witchhunting (witness Grandier and the devils of Loudon) and is not yet by any means defunct. It goes without saying that this collective projection has render-

---

[15]The analogy is rather that of counsel for the prosecution or even, perhaps, the police force. See E. Jacob, *Theology of the Old Testament,* trans. A. W. Heathcote and P. J. Allcock (New York: Harper & Brothers, 1958). pp. 70-72.

ed more difficult the dangerous but necessary task of coming to terms with the dark side of the psychic planet, of integrating the shadow and of humanizing eros.

It will be clear that so far we have demonstrated, at the most, a negative point: that in breaking away from the mythical world of meanings, the worshipers of Yahweh cleared the way for a genuinely human understanding of the erotic and its role in society. Also, that their history shows the difficulty of maintaining a truly human and personal holding-point at the center of the many tensions built into sexuality. To have desacralized and demystified sexuality was in itself no mean feat; after all, we still have the same task to perform today in a culture so vastly different from that of the ancient Near East. But now we have to go on to ask what came of it, and in order to answer this question we must first go back to our point of departure in the rejection of the divine sexual partnership. If we do so, the first thing we must note is that in Israel the relation between the god and the group is articulated in terms of familial and sexual relationship. This leads on to something of great interest for our inquiry.

In the earliest traditions and the prophetic writings, Israel is represented as the firstborn son of Yahweh. Moses is to tell Pharaoh that "Israel is my firstborn son," and, faithful to the tradition, Hosea speaks of Yahweh loving Israel his child and calling him out of Egypt (Hos. 11:1). There is, of course, no question here of Yahweh as a begetter-god; this we have already excluded. But neither is there implied the *faute de mieux* of Israel as the adopted son of Yahweh (Ezekiel represents Israel as the adopted daughter of Yahweh but she later becomes his bride and this is where the emphasis is). What comes to language here is something of a different order from either alternative. In the last analysis, fatherhood or any other familial relationship is brought about by language, the language of acknowledgment, recognition, and response, by the calling of a name. In early Hebrew society, for example, the child only becomes the father's son in the legal and true sense when the father takes him upon his knee—the symbolic language of recognition. It was said earlier that in biblical tradition man exists as response. Israel owed its existence to the fact of having been addressed as "son." We may even say that the calling of names—"father," "son"— is a reciprocal bringing into existence, since only in this way does Yahweh begin to exist as god-for-Israel, freed from the nonbeing of the demonic. At the deepest level, both Israel and Yahweh exist only by virtue of this new relationship expressed in the covenantal, that is, relational language found throughout the tradition.

What we are preparing to state here is that there is coming into sight, following on this new and intuitive language, an expression of sexuality in terms of genuine relationship liberated from the determinism and slave-dimension expressed in the myths. We should note, too, that this goes beyond the institutionalized forms of sexual relationships prevalent at that time, in particular, the dominative and therefore exploitative marriage relationship.

The first thing to note is that the emancipation of Israel (at least in principle) from the mythical prototypes resulted in a great freedom in expressing the new kind of relationship to the deity. So we find—with differing degrees of emphasis to be sure—not only father-son and father-daughter but also mother-son and husband-wife. In the Song of Moses, for example, we find a surprising reference to "the god who gave you birth" (Deut. 32:18), and more than once in the prophets we find the analogy of the mother who consoles her son or who cannot forget him to whom she gave the breast. In this way of speaking, we find something characterisitc of the prophets which does not occur elsewhere in the religious language of antiquity—a breaking apart of the old religious categories and stereotypes, a groping for a new language not so much to express what is already there but rather to bring into being a possibility only half-guessed at. The allegories of Ezekiel in which he speaks of the adoption

and betrothal of the abandoned girl-child, precisely because they are allegories, are more conscious and detached and therefore further removed from the creative point of breakthrough. The newness and creativity only emerge clearly when we pass from the basic familial relations (father, mother, child) to that between man and woman as sexual partners. Here we have a language so original and extraordinary that we must go on to look at it a little more closely.

As far as we can tell from the extant "literary debris," the point of entry of this kind of language was the personal experience of Hosea, prophet of the Northern Kingdom of Samaria, who spoke during the latter part of the eighth century before Christ. A great many theories exist, which we need not detail here, as to the form this experience took. Let us assume for the moment that he married, and his wife subsequently left him to become a temple prostitute, perhaps in the state sanctuary of Bethel. In favor of this interpretation is the fact that the role of temple prostitute points directly to the mythical theme of the sacred marriage and therefore to the bold transformation of this theme which we find in this book. Gomer stands for the land (a feminine noun in Hebrew) and the three children with their symbolic names, for the children of Israel in their progressive distancing from the covenant-relationship. The parallelism is worked out in a variety of ways throughout the book with considerable insight and skill. While it is true that the prophet is concerned in the first place with the broken covenant between Yahweh and Israel, precisely because the disclosure takes place within the area of sexual experience, it reveals a depth and dimension in sexual response for which neither the religious thinking nor the sociological realities of that time remotely prepare us. What we have here is not just the analogy of a broken marriage taken up as a useful starting point and then left behind. The thinking is carried through to the end on two levels which are mutually interactive and illuminating at all points.

The covenant between God and the people corresponds to

that between man and woman as sexual partners. "Covenant" is a juridical and political term borrowed from the language of international politics. But it is also a relational term in the most deeply personal and affective sense, which is not limited to the covenant of marriage as we see from the covenant of friendship between David and Jonathan.

What characterizes the divine covenant must also characterize that between man and woman: steadfast love, mutual compassion (suffering with the other), intimacy, and ready response. Terms denoting communication, address, and response occur with considerable frequency in Hosea. In this kind of covenant, the partners are committed to a life of mutual addressing, a calling of each other into fuller being, a mutual discovery of the one in the other.

As is clear from the description of the new covenant promised implicitly in Hosea (2:19-20) and explicitly in Jeremiah (31:31-34), mutual addressing and responding, giving and receiving, have for their final end the knowledge of Yahweh. The point has often been made that for the Hebrew knowledge is experiential rather than speculative. To know something is to have direct experience of it—"you have known the soul of an alien." To know someone means to relate as person to person. The same verb is also used of intimate sexual knowledge, either homosexual or heterosexual. In the light of these brief data, we can grasp the boldness of thinking which led Hosea, after speaking of what kind of a covenant is promised, to go on to say that "you will know the Lord." For the orgiastic religion of Canaan, sexual intercourse was the way to union with the deity, the source of life wherever it was found. Implied in the prophet's words is the liberation of the sex act from this kind of mysticism and its location in the context of an ongoing dialogue, a mutual self-giving between man and woman.

It is sometimes said that the unique and original element in

Hosea is the representation of divine love as human, of *agape* as *eros*. But, as we noted earlier, no distinction is made in the Old Testament between these two kinds of love. Moreover, it is very misleading to introduce into a discussion of Hosea's message two Greek words so loaded with meaning and presuppositions. One and the same verb, *ahav*, is used of God's love for his people and of the love which man and woman give each other in their bodies. The substantive *hesed* (generally "steadfast love" in the *Revised Standard Version*) is not a different kind of love from *ahavah* but rather its principal characteristic, and so Yahweh can say, "I have loved you with an everlasting love [*ahavah*]; therefore I have continued my faithfulness [*hesed*] to you" (Jer. 31:3). Entirely in keeping with this, there is no word in Hebrew for "sexual love" as distinct from any other kind and, for that matter, no word for "sex" either. The implication is that nowhere are sexual attraction and love isolated from the person in the totality of his relationships. Nor is any essential distinction made between divine and human love but only a spelling out of what perfect love involves.

A further indication of the profound insight of Hosea is the overcoming of the dominative and proprietary understanding of marriage current at that time in Israel and the world in which it belonged. As is clear from various prescriptions in the law codes and from the description of actual marriages, the wife was, in effect, the property of the husband—in fact, the word for "husband" in Hebrew means in the first place "proprietor," "lord." Correlative with this, the dominant pattern for the relation between the god and the people was, as recent research has shown, the unequal treaty between a suzerain and his vassal. This model of husband-wife relationship should not be too difficult for us to grasp since it has continued into modern times and is still operative in some parts of the world (as recently as 1891 we hear it proclaimed in an English court of law that the husband "has power and dominion over his wife and may keep her by force within the bounds of duty and may beat her, but not in a violent or cruel manner"!).[16] The remarkable thing is that to speak of the man-woman relationship in terms of mutual response and self-giving, a life of genuine sharing, a mutual discovery in each other, involved going beyond the institutional pattern. There is, of course, the fact documented in Hosea and elsewhere in the Old Testament, that divorce was a man's law. To the formula of covenant-annulment "you are not my people and I am not your god" (1:9) corresponds the formula of divorce pronounced by the man, "she is not my wife, and I am not her husband" (2:2). Also, we cannot help noting with distaste that the man buys the wife back for a fixed sum of money with a few other things thrown in (3:1). What, however, we might easily miss is that, in taking back the unfaithful wife, the prophet actually breaks the law which forbade precisely this (Deut. 24:1-4). Correspondingly, God is prepared to break his own law in order to restore the broken relationship. Here we have a hint, not often detected, of the new relationship which will rest not on obedience to law and the lawgiver but on the sole impulse of the heart (Jer. 31:31-34).

No special pleading is required to point out the irreplaceable significance of this way of thinking for our situation today. The demythologizing and desacralizing of sexuality cannot be achieved once for all but has to be fought for all the time. The overcoming of the demonic and dominative—the slave-dimension in human sexual relations—is a struggle which has to be undertaken by every individual and every society and at the heart of the struggle is the issue of freedom. In Hebrew tradition even God is involved in this struggle since it is his freedom also which is at stake. That Hosea and consequently also Yahweh break the law concerning a divorced woman, that the paradigms here presented go beyond the sociological realities of that time, in particular the institution of marriage, warn us

---

[16]Quoted in Alex Comfort, *Sex in Society* (New York: Citadel Press, 1966), pp. 88ff.

against absolutizing either law, convention, or social institutions in evaluating sexual response. Does this mean that *eros* is free of law and a law to itself? Let us see whether the tradition can help us to answer this question or at least clarify it.

3

LAW OR LOVE?

The possibility which exists today of sex safe from the three-fold danger of infection, conception, and detection has shown up the prudential and shallow nature of much of traditional church teaching on sexuality and sexual conduct. In a relatively new environment of freedom, it has been clear for some time that the mandate of the churches to dictate norms is no longer widely regarded. The sequel to *Humanae Vitae* has shown, what was already obvious to the more perceptive, that sexual standards can no longer be dictated by ecclesiastical decree. Since the parental mandate is rapidly going the same way, "law" is reduced, in effect, to the civil law which operates as a deterrent only against such extreme instances of antisocial sexual behavior as rape, but is more doubtful in borderline cases such as abortion and pornography. Since most people can operate comfortably within the limits of the civil law and since even the negative commands of the decalogue proscribe only "possible courses of action which lie at the edges of the sphere of human life,"[1] it really boils down to the question of criteria for evaluating sexual conduct within limits defined by the law.

It would not be difficult to point out, especially in the Roman Catholic setting, how unrealistic rules of conduct and guidelines have been and to what extent the options have been narrowed down. The supposition seems to be that realism is in order in politics and the conduct of business but not in sex which admits of no *parvitas materiae*. In general, it would not be unfair to

---

[1]Gerhard von Rad, *Old Testament Theology,* trans. D. M. G. Stalker, 2 vols. (New York: Harper & Row, 1962-1966), 2:391.

say that this lack of realism and imagination, and not just in Roman Catholicism, has played no small part in producing the sexual schizophrenia and hypocrisy against which the Benjamin Braddocks (*The Graduate*) of today are rebelling. If the churches are to have any criteriological role in our society, in which the only constant factor seems to be change, they must present some persuasive theological basis for evaluating thinking and practice in this area, and the question must be asked whether they have the resources to carry out this task.

We only have to look at the situation today to see the enormous difficulties involved. Appeal can no longer be made to the "authority" of the Bible and church tradition, since most people no longer ask what are the divinely ordained rules telling them what to do in any given situation. Moreover, the churchman's past seems to tell against him. Ecclesiastical professionals have elaborated theologies of marriage, attempted to define what is permissible within the marriage bond, how far one may "go" in sexual friendship whether eventuating in marriage or not, how the birth of children may or may not be regulated, and so on. Much of this has been burdened not only by lack of realism and of that creative imagination which is somewhere at the roots of moral perception but also by archaic anthropological ideas and dated exegesis. If the role of the churches is to go anywhere beyond supplementing and at times challenging civil legislation, they have to speak of a Christian understanding of eroticism as such, and this, so far, they have not done.

In view of the widespread feeling that we now have a totally new situation and environment in which the old rules and standards no longer apply, it may seem hazardous to suggest that we look back into the past, especially the Christian past, for guidelines. Let us begin by admitting, as we must, that a good part of that past is *merely* past, that is, archaic, and can no more be brought up into the air we breathe than some ancient objet d'art uncovered by the archeologist's spade. Yet, it would be naive just the same to think that this past and this tradition have no bearing on the present task of moral evaluation. To dispel this idea, it would be sufficient to note that the analyst is concerned in the first place with dissolving an inauthentic sense of guilt which his client has inherited from his own past, which in its turn has been deeply colored by the cultural and religious values of his parents and of the whole milieu in which he was formed. At the very least, therefore, we have the duty of getting the past off our backs, of unburdening, which involves awareness that the past is still subtly and invisibly with us.

This brings us to the admission that just as a good part of our individual moral conscience is archaic and therefore a hindrance to development, so much of what we who still call ourselves Christians have inherited from the Christian past inhibits our coming to terms as Christians with the present situation. At the very least, therefore, we are involved in a work of exorcism, getting rid of "the rotted past,"[2] dissolving a collective superego which has absorbed attitudes and values of the past that collect like ghosts and shadows wherever they can find a place to congregate. And, to pursue the metaphor, this kind of demon goes out only when we give it a name, bring it out into the open, see and understand it for what it is.

To take this a little further, we should recall the widely held view that the unfocused sense of guilt which seems inseparable from sexual experience in our culture derives from the parental prohibition interiorized in the parasitic stage and eventuated later in an ethic based on law-observance and obedience to the Great Parent. Freud complained that the association between sexuality and guilt has been much promoted by Jewish and Christian monotheism, a nomistic approach to sexuality characteristic of both traditions, and the Christian doctrine of Original Sin, especially in its Augustinian formulation. Though often questioned (especially by Jews and Christians), this thesis has

---

[2]I take this term from my colleague at Chicago Theological Seminary, Professor Ross Snyder.

been very influential and has inspired works as different as Hesnard's *Moralité sans Péché*, Sauty's *Psychoanalyse et Religion* and Erich Fromm's widely read *Psychoanalysis and Religion*.[3] The point is that both Jew and Christian, precisely because they are within this tradition, come to consciousness in different degrees of clarity and intensity as *accused*. The thesis would certainly seem to find support in the figures of Alexander Portnoy and Stephen Daedalus. Both are involved in an interminable and unsuccessful struggle for exoneration, the former on Dr. Spielvogel's couch, the latter in the confessional of the Jesuit fathers. This circuitry of guilt, ordeal by shame, and unsuccessful exoneration in its turn generates self-hatred, disgust, and a great deal of self-directed (and therefore other-directed) aggression. It may also help to explain the inordinate amount of violence which is obvious throughout the biblical record and the history of the Christian church.

Whether or not we regard this as a caricature, sooner or later we have to take a hard look at the form in which the Judeo-Christian tradition—the influence of which operates both on the conscious and unconscious levels—has been mediated to us. If we start our inquiry with the Jewish Scriptures, to which absolute authority has been attributed by both Jew and Christian for centuries, we might be tempted to conclude that an interpretation of these writings as authoritative and normative has, on balance, done more harm than good. To stay on the level of conscious motivation and influence (the unconscious can be verified by a glance into the case histories of any psychoanalyst), we might consider attitudes toward the homosexual. It has often been pointed out by those who ought to know that the violent antipathy which many feel towards the homosexual, even when not guilty of any "criminal" offense, has a great deal to do with

---

[3] Dr. Hesnard, *Moralité sans Péché* (Paris: Presses Universitaires, 1954); Roger Sauty, *Psychoanalyse et Religion. Etude psychanalytique, philosophique et théologique des grands problèmes religieux*, (Geneva, 1961); E. Fromm, *Psychoanalysis and Religion* (Ithaca, N. Y.: Yale University Press, 1950).

repressed and unacknowledged homosexual tendencies in the accuser. A person sure of his sexual identity more naturally would feel pity than anger. In a sense, therefore, the accusation is a technique of exoneration. It can be demonstrated historically that the death penalty for homosexual practice in European civil codes, beginning with that of Justinian, was strongly influenced by Old Testament legislation (Lev. 18:22; 20:13) and the story of Sodom and Gomorrah. By now it is widely known that from the exegetical viewpoint, the inference was hardly legitimate. The Old Testament legislation had in view the practice of cultic male prostitution (whatever they may have thought of noncultic homosexual practice), and the Cities of the Plain were destroyed as much for violation of the age-old duty of hospitality as for addiction to "unnatural vice." The systems of literary interpretation applied to biblical texts in the pre-scientific period allowed both Jew and Christian to find in these and similar texts almost anything they wished to find. Philo, for example, reads into the story of the two cities the vice of pederasty so common in his own milieu; Jerome freely edited texts to fit his own views on sexual morality; and medieval moralists threatened monastery and royal court with the fate which befell the unsuspecting cities. Beyond a doubt, all of this helped delay the advent of humanitarian legislation and contributed to the widespread insistence that the homosexual be dragged into the open and punished. It is a sobering thought that the death penalty for male homosexuality was abolished in Britain as recently as 1861.[4]

Other examples could be given. The sixth and ninth commandments of the decalogue have been taken out of context and made the basis for an all-encompassing and oppressive sexual ethic. A one-sided, proprietary, and patriarchal model of sexual partnership, common not only in the Old Testament but throughout the ancient Near East, has been proposed as the ideal for

---

[4]For this whole question see D. Sherwin Bailey, *Homosexuality and the Western Christian Tradition* (New York: Hillary House, 1955).

Christian marriage. The means by which Onan, son of Judah, avoided his social responsibility has been appealed to abusively time out of number in order to impress on the young the grave sinfulness of masturbation, thus establishing a "divine" sanction which has delayed a genuinely therapeutic approach to this very human problem and caused untold anguish. The priestly laws of ritual purity, not unconnected with ancient taboos, have been conscripted to bolster legislation making clerical celibacy mandatory, thus obscuring a genuinely and specifically Christian approach to celibacy. The result has been that for very many people Christianity, far from being an experience of joy and liberation, has been turned into a burden unwillingly borne, an experience in which guilt and self-rejection play a dominant role—to all intents and purposes an education to self-hatred.

We could hardly leave this subject without referring to the "double standard" fostered throughout Christian history on the basis of biblical authority. This has been so thoroughly discussed that it would be tiresome to enlarge on it here but one aspect at least ought to be touched on. Throughout history divorce legislation has always been the litmus test for the relative status of the sexes, and in Old Testament legislation divorce is very clearly a man's law. That no provision is ever made for the protection of the woman in the event of the marital infidelity of her partner (though the death penalty was prescribed for both parties in adultery) is hardly surprising in view of the decided inferiority of the woman in early Semitic society. The patriarchal view of marriage implied that the husband was the proprietor of the wife and could exercise proprietary rights over her. As is clear from the wording of the prohibition against coveting in the decalogue, the woman is thought of as an extension of the man's personality together with his other effects.

The well-known passage of Deuteronomy 24:1-4, to which the Pharisees appealed in their question addressed to Jesus about divorce (Mt. 19:3-9), is not a divorce law at all, though Jerome

mistranslated it as such. It merely prescribed the correct pro-
cedure in the event of separation having taken place and at the
same time illustrates the flimsy grounds on which a wife could
be divorced (if the husband finds "some indecency" in her or
simply gets to dislike her). Down to New Testament times, a
man could, according to some authorities, send his wife pack-
ing even if she did not turn out to be a good cook.

It may be true that prophetic thinking transcended this in-
equality as it transcended other stipulations of the law. Yet, in
a sense Hosea perpetuated it by transposing the covenant relationship between unequal partners into marital terms. God,
after all, precisely because he is God, could annul his part of
the covenant on the grounds of the infidelity of Israel, his
spouse; whereas Israel was hardly in a position to challenge him.
Yet, we do hear in Hosea that a new relationship will come into
existence within which the male god will be addressed no longer
as "my lord" but "my man," as husband in the true sense of
the word (Hos. 2:16). Unfortunately, however, this insight
was not followed up due to the apparently endemic tendency
to grasp at the legal and overlook the prophetic. This tendency
has been very influential in maintaining the double standard
right down to the present, and has been much abetted by the
wide acceptance of the interpretation (sometimes misinterpretation) of some crucial texts in the Pauline letters.

It might not be out of place to recall at this point that what
Christians appeal to as the Old Testament was first, and still
remains, the sacred Scriptures of Judaism, and that Judaism
has drawn from this source conclusions for the evaluation of
sexual conduct often quite different from those accepted by
Christians. Judaism, for example, never has accepted the
ascetical ideal, never has advocated celibacy (except in very
rare cases and for quite different reasons) and never has had
monks.[5] There never has appeared in mainstream Judaism

---

[5] If we choose to consider Essenes and the men of Qumran as monks
we have to bear in mind that they were not part of the mainstream.

any tendency to disparage sexual partnership in marriage or to regard "the flesh" as prone to evil. On the contrary, a person who remained unmarried was generally regarded as suspect or at least highly unfortunate. We find in the Talmud a saying which must seem very surprising, if not shocking, to the conventional Christian: "a man is to give account in the hereafter for any permissible pleasure from which he has abstained."[6] Jewish teachers have spoken of the "evil impulse" in man, but this never has amounted to anything like the doctrine of Original Sin.

Freud thought that Hebrew and Jewish law observance represented a collective superego. He interpreted it as a substitute satisfaction for instinctual pleasure based on the expectation of being loved the more by God. But this theory hardly does justice to the evidence. We now know what Freud did not, that Hebrew law codes are not significantly different for the most part from other ancient Semitic collections and come closest to them in legislation concerning sexual conduct. Freud, apparently accepted the Graf-Wellhausen hypothesis that the eighth century prophets were the originators not only of monotheism but of the substance of the law (at least they rediscovered Egyptian monotheism). This thesis, now abandoned, would seem to imply that both law and prophets come out strongly against sexual sin and instinctual pleasure in general. Before examining whether this is in fact the case, we might first look at certain other commonly held suppositions about the laws, especially the negative commands, in the Old Testament. Though not immediately apparent, some of these play a significant role in the current debate between exponents of a situation ethic and those who argue that rules still are relevant to the moral decisions of the Christian.

The traditional view, still cherished by fundamentalists, is that the law codes in the Old Testament, particularly the deca-

---

[6]Jerusalem Talmud, *Kiddushin,* 4.12. Quoted from Isidore Epstein, *Judaism* (Baltimore: Penguin Pelican Book, 1959), p. 156.

logue, were delivered to Moses by God at a particular point in time and thereafter promulgated to the entire community. Before the beginning of this century, there was some excuse for thinking that these law codes were unique both in their origin and content. Now that we have at least half a dozen complete or fragmentary law codes from the ancient Near Eastern area, of which the best known is that of Hammurabi discovered in 1901, this view is no longer possible. With perhaps only one exception all of these collections antedate the Hebrew law codes, and of course the individual prescriptions generally will antedate the collection of which they form part. A comparative study of this vast ensemble of customary law leads to the conclusion that in no case do such collections come into existence at one precise moment of time. Customary law comes into existence in response to the needs of a particular community at different stages of its development. The promulgation of a code like that of Napoleon, of course, may be dated, but the stipulations which it contains in nearly every case have a long history behind them. The Old Testament laws reflect the existence throughout many centuries of the Israelite community. They came into existence in response to the needs of that community, and their primary function, as with law in general, was to prevent its dissolution.[7] Obvious as it is, this observation at once removes some of the pejorative aura surrounding the concept of law in much of the discussion which is going on today. Ideally at least, law is a deposit of the collective wisdom of a particular community with regard to what is essential to its own existence and, in particular, to the setting of limits. Viewed in this light, the light of its origins, law cannot be put in absolute antithesis to freedom since freedom without limits is meaningless. The intrinsic association between law and community purely as a historical datum raises some ques-

---

[7]See the treatment of the laws in M. Noth, *The Laws in the Pentateuch and Other Essays*, trans. D. R. Ap-Thomas (Philadelphia: Fortress Press, 1967), pp. 1-107.

tions for the proponents of an ethic of the situation. It is quite a question, for example, whether these writers escape the charge of taking for granted the ethos of middle-class liberalism with its emphasis on the individual over against society and its tendency to concentrate attention on sexual conduct.

Once we accept that the Old Testament laws did not come into existence in a cultural vacuum, it becomes clear that many commonly held assumptions about them have to be rejected. It is no longer possible, for example, to suppose that they contain some kind of revolutionary social ethic. The humanitarian provisions found here and there, especially in Deuteronomy—care for widows, the fatherless, aliens, and unemployed clergy—are not by any means unique and have to be taken together with other provisions such as the death penalty for striking or cursing parents.[*] The law of retaliation ("eye for eye, tooth for tooth, wound for wound . . ."), originally a constructive measure for limiting the practice of indiscriminate revenge, does not go beyond what we find in earlier Semitic legislation. And there is nothing particularly original about the prohibition of such thing as murder, adultery, or stealing.

As for the origin of these laws, the parallels which have come to light show clearly that the attribution of law to the deity was a universal expedient for authenticating the law and giving it binding force in a particular community. There is really little difference between King Hammurabi receiving the famous law code from the hands of the sun-god (as depicted on the famous stele in the Louvre) and Moses going up the mountain to receive the covenant law from the hands of Yahweh. In both cases the representation comes from the community, which accepts the laws. It expresses not only esteem for the law but also a sense of its own primordiality as a community and what

---

[*]This was not directed primarily at children but rather the younger members of the larger family of the clan. Calvin's literal (mis)interpretation of this text resulted in the execution of at least one child in Geneva; a further and particularly tragic example of what unsound hermeneutics can lead to.

it believes to be the source of its own existence. In neither case can it easily be argued that the law was thought of as the arbitrary imposition on the community of an alien will in the form of prescriptions and proscriptions contained in the law.

The decalogue has always been accorded a privileged status in the Jewish and Christian traditions. Voices can still be heard from Christian pulpits insisting that it is binding on the Christian in its entirety, and we have seen how the sixth and ninth stipulations have been made the basis for instruction on sexual morality at least in the Catholic tradition. In view of this, it may be difficult to accept that what has been said of law in general is true also of these solemn prohibitions.

The fact that there are *ten* does not derive from some mysterious religious premise. All it does is indicate a certain stage in the development and arrangement of individual legal pronouncements, as is clear from similar collections of ten or twelve in the Old Testament." Even a casual reading of the two versions in Exodus and Deuteronomy will show clear indications of development within this particular series. The sabbath law, for example, is justified in the one version on humanitarian grounds, in the other with reference to a theological or doctrinal premise. That they are all couched in the negative, apodictic form may well indicate, moreover, that these more general norms represent a distillation of ancient customary law and were put together for recital by the community in a service of worship. Therefore, it could be seen as part of the process by which customary law was reduced to general norms of conduct, a process which was furthered by prophetic preaching and continued in the rabbinical schools and by Jesus himself.

All that has been said so far would apply to the various laws which concern sexual conduct. In no significant respect are they different from what we find elsewhere in the ancient Near East. In fact, Hebrew law in this area probably comes closer to other Semitic legislation than anywhere else. It is unfortunate,

---

"For example, Ex. 34:14-26 and Deut. 27:15-26.

if in a way inevitable, that much has been made throughout
the Christian tradition of the sexual prohibitions found in the
legislation, since this results in a distortion of the total intent
of the law and, in many cases, a positive misrepresentation of
its meaning. The obvious example is the practice, referred
to earlier, of taking the sixth and ninth prohibitions of the
decalogue out of their context, thus placing the emphasis on
sexual irregularity as such, rather than on violation of personal
rights and of the social order. That the prohibition of adultery
comes between murder and stealing ("kidnapping" would probably be the original sense here) points clearly in this direction,
and we might recall that David's adultery with Bathsheba is
represented as stealing (2 Sam. 12, cf. Prov. 6:29-31). The
same emphasis is apparent in laws concerning rape, which,
incidentally, are practically identical with provisions in Meso-
potamian legislation. The rape of a girl neither married nor
betrothed carried only the penalty of marrying the wronged
party without further option, together with payment of a fine,
whereas in every other case the penalty was death—for both
parties if it was established that the woman could have sought
help and did not.[10]

What we are saying here is something very simple: that
law is a necessity of social life and that rather than viewing
it as a limitation of freedom we ought to think of it as fostering
freedom by indicating limits beyond which freedom becomes
meaningless because it is unrelational. This does not of course
imply that law is an absolute datum. Bad laws should be
resisted and obsolete laws repealed; in fact, we can trace this
process of adaptation throughout Israelite history (compare,
for example, the ancient covenant code in Exodus 20:22-23,33
with Deuteronomy 12-26). In sexual matters the Israelite laws
touch only on what concerns the rights of the person. At the
same time, there is some point to Freud's accusation, not in
the laws themselves but in what both Jews and Christians have

---

[10] Deut. 22:22-27 and Lev. 20:10.

made of them. The history of Israel, especially in the later period, provides one of the best examples of how law can be transformed into an abstract entity and the meticulous observance of law into a way of life. When this happens, the law enters into collusion with the interiorized prohibition of the premoral stage. Together with the faultless carrying out of cultic actions and rubrics, it becomes a technique of exoneration, a means of exorcizing a sense of guilt which arises more naturally in sexual matters than in other areas. It can also happen that by reducing justice to the level of law observance, the "just man" succeeds in limiting the demand made on him by love of and regard for his neighbor. This is clearly one of the principal aspects of Jesus' polemic against the Pharisees.

If the law does not place any particular emphasis on sexual sin, neither do the prophets. Wherever sexual sin is denounced, the accent is never on abandonment to instinctual pleasure but on possessiveness and the violation of the person and his rights. Paul Ricoeur has made this point very persuasively in his review of the previously mentioned book of Dr. Hesnard. He points out that the prophetic accusation is, in Freudian terms, an attack less on the "id" than on the "superego" itself. In other words, the prophetic accusation is directed at what passes for religion—including cultic and legal observances in which it is objectified as a means of self-exoneration—and brings the justice of God down to man's level. What is at stake in the prophetic challenge is the recognition of man as man, which, in the words of Paul Ricoeur, implies that "the individual is torn away from an obscure and solitary battle with his instincts and placed on the great stage of the world." Ricoeur continues:

> Biblical sin is in no sense centered on sexuality; the prophets include it among the relations of covetousness and possession in regard to others. This aspect is further accentuated by the teaching and attitude of Jesus: the prostitute only needs to break a bottle of perfume but the young rich man must give away everything. This is because evil chiefly involves hardness of heart; in

this respect money is more evil than sex, since it wounds more deeply the capacity to accept others. Thus even in sexual morality the prophets' accent is not Oedipian; it is not pleasure as such which is suspect but the monopoly, the avariciousness, the slave dimension of human sexuality. Oedipian premorality is anti-hedonist; prophetic morality is anti-possessive.[11]

In a sense, this does not represent a new departure since the law, right from the beginning, had been presented in the context of covenant-relationship, that is, in relational terms. Failure to recognize this has been chiefly responsible for the calumny that Judaism is essentially legalistic, a calumny which, we suspect, owes something to Paul's dichotomy between law and freedom in Christ, a dichotomy born in the heat of a fierce polemic. The prophets were familiar with the law, preached it, and condemned their contemporaries for not observing it. What, however, we observe in the prophetic writings is a twofold tendency: to stress that truly relational existence to which the law points, and to reduce the individual stipulations of the law to general principles (as in Mic. 6:8) and ultimately to the one principle which alone gives the law its meaning and function—the principle of creative love and concern for the other.

Does this imply that prophetic thinking tended to supersede the law and point to a state or condition in which there would be no place for it? We would be inclined to think that the prophets attribute to the law a negative but necessary function, and that they insist that it cannot be absolutized or used to limit the demand made upon each by the neighbor. Though they do cite particular violations of the law—Hosea 4:1-2 and Jeremiah 7:9 obviously refer to the decalogue, for example—what they condemn basically are false attitudes. When Amos condemns those who recline on ivory beds but are not grieved over the impending ruin of the state (Amos 6:4-6), he is not

---

[11]Review of Dr. Hesnard, *Moralité sans Péché*, in *Espirit*, August-September, 1954, translated in *Cross Currents*, Vol. 5, No. 4, pp. 346-7.

talking about specific laws since there were no laws forbidding anyone lying on ivory beds or eating lambs of the flock or singing idle songs. What he is condemning is an attitude of mind by which a person simply does not care enough about other people to get involved. Whether this implies, as Joseph Fletcher seems to suggest,[12] that the prophets were situationists, is another matter. There is certainly no indication that they pitted an all-embracing apprehension of love or covenant-fidelity against law. What they constantly emphasize is the limitless love by virtue of which the law was given in the first place and, correspondingly, the limitless demand of love and concern for neighbor. When they castigate their contemporaries for failure to observe the law, they are speaking of limits beyond which no love or concern is possible. For the man who—in Heschel's phrase—is in sympathy with the divine pathos, the law in its negative function has been left far behind. The future Israel, the remnant, will be composed of those who have the law written on their hearts, who have radicalized its demands and therefore can dispense with the tablets of stone (Jer. 31: 31-34). Notwithstanding all this, the prophets were too realistic even to hint at the abrogation or supersession of the law in favor of some all-embracing principle or ethical norm. They were too much aware of its societal function and of the need for limits recognized as valid by the community they were addressing. In short, it seems impossible to read into the prophetic message any dichotomy between law and love.

It would appear at first sight that the same can be said of Jesus, whose ethical teaching, insofar as we can reconstruct it, is in direct line of succession to that of the great prophets. But before we can say anything about the ethical teaching or consciousness of Jesus, we have to presuppose that, despite all the difficulties involved, it is possible to get behind the traditional

---

[12]Joseph Fletcher, *Situation Ethics* (Philadelphia: Westminster, 1966), p. 19. I do not find the phrase "an understanding of the situation" in the references which Fletcher gives at this point to Heschel's *The Prophets*.

communities of the first century to a mission, a life-style, and an experience which for them were normative. Of course, this does not justify us in regarding either the New Testament as a whole or the Gospels in particular as a source book for Christian ethics. But neither does it exclude the possibility of searching for clues to fundamental moral attitudes which can inform the decisions we are called upon to make in our own situation. The temptation of fastening on to sayings of Jesus as infallible guides to moral conduct must be put aside, of course, from the start. Apart from the hermeneutical and exegetical difficulties involved in this still widespread practice, it contradicts the basic prophetic and charismatic attitude presupposed throughout the Gospels by subjugating the spirit to the letter. Some of the difficulties involved in reading the Gospels as a source book of "Christian morality" will be appreciated if we recall that Jesus broke his own injunctions against anger, turning the other cheek, and using the epithet "fool."[13] More serious in its consequences has been the widespread, conviction that the answer of Jesus to the Pharisees about divorce (Mt. 19:9) excludes the possibility of this option at all times and in all circumstances. A great deal of writing, mostly one-sided and polemical, has been done on the so-called exceptive clause. But even if you satisfy yourself that the clause is not exceptive, you really have not proved very much. Jesus reaffirms the primordial sacrality of the man-woman relationship over against its historical vagaries by appealing to the first state of man in relation to woman (Gen. 2:24). God's purpose in marriage is demonstrated with reference to creation. But can this be taken as a *legal* statement binding under all circumstances? How can it be known that God has joined a man and woman together so that they have become "one flesh"? To take this view would involve falling into the same legalistic mind-set castigated by Jesus himself.

---

[13]Cf. Mt. 5:21-22 with Ch. 23, especially v. 17, and Mt. 5:39 with Jn. 18:23.

It is clearly out of the question to suppose that Jesus proposed a new law in place of the old, and no one in the early church, with the possible exception of Hermas (who came from a legalistic, Essene-type Judaism), imagined that he did. Wherever we meet the phrase "the law of Christ" or something similar, the reference is always to liberty or the Spirit or love and concern for the neighbor. But having dispelled this false assumption, we are faced with the problem of Jesus' attitude to the old law, the Torah. On the basis of the extant Jesus-tradition, it seems very difficult to argue that he regarded this law as nonoperative in the new situation created by his appearance and preaching. Even when castigating the hypocrisy of the scribes and Pharisees, the "just men" of his day, he enjoined his disciples to put into practice the law which the Pharisees preached but did not practice (Mt. 23:3). And we must not forget what he said about the law standing "until all is accomplished" (Mt. 5:18).

What is significant is not so much the relevance and centrality of the Torah for Jesus, which we would have expected in the context of that time, but his attitude toward it. In the passage in which he blasts the Pharisees with the scorn of his invective, he never blames them for fulfilling the law but for exploiting it for their own ends, using it as a means of self-exoneration leading to forgetfulness of justice, mercy, and faith—"the weightier matters of the law" (Mt. 23:23). In other words, the law retains its function only when it points beyond itself to the positive claim made upon me by the other, a claim which is without limit and which, therefore, cannot be circumscribed by any law. It is for this reason that Jesus could make the startling and paradoxical statement that the righteousness of these, the most righteous of all righteous men, would not carry them into the kingdom, and that the harlots and quislings would get there before them.

In these and other sayings attributed to Jesus, especially those in the first Gospel, we have to allow for the influence of

polemical attitudes and therefore of a certain *odium theologicum* in the experience of early Christian communities, which had come into existence in a Jewish milieu. Neglect of this important factor and, in general, of the thought-world of Judaism at that time might lead us to think that the attitude of Jesus vis-à-vis the Torah was in every respect unique, and this is certainly not true. Jesus sums up all the demands of the law in the one commandment of love, but so did other rabbis at that time. As is clear from the series of "Woes" in Matthew 23, his accusation against the Pharisees was not so much that they were legalists but that they sought after "smooth things" by means of casuistry and thereby eviscerated the ultimate demand contained in the law; and this complaint was made by others in the world of Judaism at the time.[14] In the episode of the plucking of wheat on the sabbath and the sayings about pure and impure foods, the perceptive among Jesus' audience may well have felt a new principle in operation. But at no point did Jesus abrogate the specific demands of· Hebrew law with regard to sexuality or anything else.

We might clarify the situation by saying that for Jesus the law was no longer considered a series of negative commands and that therefore law observance could no longer be proposed as a way of life. Fulfilment is traced back to the heart where generosity and avarice, concern and possessiveness divide. None of the prohibitions of the decalogue concerns "internal acts"—not even that of coveting which, in the context, means laying hands on the property of another. For Jesus, however, destructive anger is the moral equivalent of murder and lust the moral equivalent of adultery. The disciples are pressed to reach the point of genuine interiority with regard to the demands of the law, which implies that law observance elevated to a way of life, as with the Pharisees, was in itself symptomatic of a failure which had already taken place. This approach not

---

[14]See M. Black and H. H. Rowley, *Peake's Commentary on the Bible* (Camden, N. J.: Thomas Nelson, 1962), p. 776.

only freed the basic demand of the law from the smoke screen of casuistry but made it possible for Jesus to take up a very free and charismatic attitude to the individual stipulations of the law.

Despite the scarcity of material and the formidable warnings of form critics, we cannot help noting a certain directness, lack of system, and especially human realism in Jesus' attitude to moral questions. People are evaluated not by what they say or profess but by what they do and the kind of people they are—"by their fruits you shall know them." This realism dissolves all the legal pilpul about how far you can walk on the sabbath or whether you can pull off a few ears of wheat when crossing a field (also on the sabbath) or what kinds of food you can eat and when. It is not a cold, detached kind of realism or that other kind which is often appealed to when a moral decision is about to be sidestepped. On the contrary, the kind of realism we are speaking of here leads to acceptance of others as they are, not as we think they ought to be; it is, therefore, a positive and creative quality. A good example may be found in the incident of the adulteress brought before Jesus by the Pharisees to provide a pretext for outwitting him in a scholastic debate. They referred to the law (not quite accurately in fact) and asked him what they ought to do. Instead of entering into the spirit of the debate, Jesus did a remarkably nonconsequential thing, a prophetic gesture or perhaps a nongesture; he bent down and started writing or just doodling in the dust, interrupting himself only to straighten up and say, "let him who is without sin among you be the first to throw a stone at her." This sudden *argumentum ad hominem*, characteristic of the prophets, was enough to kill the debate before it ever got started. The adultery is not condoned, but the woman is accepted as she is, in her real personhood and not as a pawn in a game played by moral theologians. This attitude of creative realism together with the steady refusal to judge is, if anything, the really new thing in the context of Judaism at that time.

The same attitude comes through on the occasion when Jesus was dining in the house of a Pharisee friend. It happened that a prostitute came in off the street and performed for him, in her own way, the office of hospitality which the host had neglected. The Pharisee betrayed his displeasure at such association with a public sinner, but Jesus characteristically replied with a parable which was also an *argumentum ad hominem*.

It is unfortunate that the concluding saying remains difficult to interpret: "her sins, which are many, are forgiven, for she loved much; but he who is forgiven little, loves little (Lk. 7: 47)." In the second line we would have expected, "he who loves little is forgiven little," indicating that love and openness are the necessary conditions for forgiveness and acceptance. What at any rate is clear is the acceptance on Jesus' part of this gesture from a person rejected by a self-righteous society. It may be of interest to add that in the parallels to this incident in the other synoptic Gospels (Mk. 14:3-9 and Mt. 26:6-13), there is no hint that the woman is a prostitute, and the emphasis is on the waste of good and expensive ointment. If we take the parallel versions together, we have an illustration of an important point made earlier in this chapter in the quotation from Paul Ricoeur: that money is more evil than sex since it wounds more deeply the capacity to accept others. It is this *capacity to accept* which seems to be for Jesus the fundamental and indispensable moral attitude.

What, then, can we say about the relation of law and love in the light of the extant tradition about "all that Jesus began to do and teach" (Acts 1:1)? The law is not abrogated since its basic demand corresponds to the very being of the God who revealed his purpose to a people. The prophetic tradition to which Jesus belongs supersedes law observance as a way of life, but there is no antithesis between law and love: "You shall therefore love the Lord your God, and keep . . . his commandments always" (Deut. 11:1); "If you love me, you will

keep my commandments" (Jn. 14:15); "A new commandment I give you, that you love one another" (Jn. 13:34). The
apparent opposition between law and love in the tradition about
Jesus is explained by the fact that so often he is addressing
and challenging people who are using law observance as a
shield against the call for genuine acceptance and concern for
the neighbor. One can speak of being free of the law only *after*
this critical point and not *before*. It is at this point that we
are challenged to clarify what we mean when we speak of being
free, in particular when we speak of being free to love.

4

FREEDOM

Today as always, the ambiguity of freedom is a central fact of experience. Freedom is desired and demanded, but its consequences are feared. We wish to be free to choose and at the same time not to be bound by the consequences of our choice; and so the call for freedom is often followed by a headlong flight from the terrifying consequences of having to decide and act for ourselves. Today more than ever, freedom is the key word for the large numbers of the alienated younger generation. Emancipation at an earlier age from parental authority and from the supportive myths of political and religious establishments is obviously to be welcomed as a necessary step to genuine personhood; but it also implies that the adolescent will experience sooner than he otherwise would some of the ambiguities involved in appealing to freedom. One aspect is brought out by a student participating in a sit-in: "You can't grow up if there are no walls to push against," he tells the reporter, "but you can't grow up either if the walls give way when you push against them." The history of freedom movements in all ages illustrates how difficult it is to translate freedom into some negotiable terms.

Used as a slogan or key word, "freedom" is generally qualified by adjectives such as political, economic, sexual. In each case it is a question of being free *from* something. Sexual freedom is understood as emancipation from parental restraint or ecclesiastical stricture or social convention with its pressure to conform. A young person might, for example, put it this way: "I am free to do as I wish so long as I stay within the law. I

63

don't see any reason why I should accept uncritically sexual standards dictated or held by my parents or minister or priest. There is a new openness among us young people today. We accept our bodies, and we know what we are doing when we get involved with another person. I may or may not decide to sleep with my girl friend whether or not we eventually get married. We know what we are doing, and the decision is ours alone. We're willing to take responsibility for our actions so why should anyone else worry?" For this attitude, which is certainly better than abject timidity or hypocrisy, the balance is delicately tipped between freedom *from* and freedom *for*. It is also true that in some circumstances—in a situation of stifling social convention, for example—it might be necessary to speak only of freedom *from*, without regard to consequences. Yet, sooner or later the ambiguity surfaces, the illusion that freedom is a quality which we can possess once and for all, that to be free it is enough to declare our independence. As Bonhoeffer put it, we think we are pushing and we are being pushed. The literature of the world, and of our own age in particular, is full of the broken illusions of those who thought that they were free.

The subject of freedom in general, and sexual freedom in particular, is especially important for the Christian in the changing situation today. "Religion" as a compulsive routine is tolerated by fewer and fewer people, dependence is no longer widely felt to be at the source of religious experience and the age-old symbols of divine authority (kingship, lordship, et cetera) are losing their appeal. We might even be tempted to think, with Nietzsche, that if God is dead, anything is permitted. In this situation it is especially important to have some idea what we mean when we talk about freedom.

Instead of beginning with someone like Camus, Sartre, or Gide, it might be original to take as a point of departure for these reflections the apparently artless story of the Man, the Woman, and the Snake near the beginning of the Book of

Genesis. As has already been pointed out, this should be read not as the work of a historian but of a wisdom teacher, as a reflection on experience inspired by faith. It is, in a way, a parable on the ambiguities of freedom. The Man is created by God, placed in a delightful garden and given the Woman as companion. The only thing forbidden him is to eat of the tree of knowledge of good and evil. Now the uncommitted reader might think this a pointless prohibition which the Man very reasonably and rightly disregarded, but there are depths below depths in this story. The impulse to disobey the command comes from the Snake, who gets into a theological conversation with the Woman and suggests new possibilities of a greatly enhanced existence once the prohibition is disregarded. Grasp at your freedom, he insinuates, and you will enjoy limitless existence, "You will be like divine beings who know good and evil." The Man and the Woman do as he says, take the decisive step beyond the command, and experience not limitless existence but shame, division, and betrayal of each other's trust.

The implications of this story must have been quite clear to the Israelite to whom it was first addressed, and to a great extent they still are clear for us. The command is the Torah, which the Israelite accepts in the context of the covenant relationship. Far from being the arbitrary imposition of an alien authority, it reveals the true meaning of freedom by indicating the limits within which alone it can be exercised meaningfully. Beyond these limits it becomes meaningless, demonic, and destructive because it is nonrelational. Nor is the sexual element, which is unmistakable, there by accident.[1] Even a casual reading of the legislation and the historical narratives of the Old Testament will reveal the fatal fascination which

---

[1] The symbolism of the Snake, the pun on the Hebrew word *'arum,* which connotes cunning and nakedness, the ambivalence of "knowledge," the Hebrew word for which also can refer to coition, the ensuing shame at nakedness. However, this does not lead necessarily to the conclusions drawn from this passage by Augustine, nor does it even presuppose that the passage describes a "fall."

the orgiastic practices of Canaan exercised on the Hebrew. His tenure of the land, as the Man's of the garden, was conditional on his remaining within the limits of a truly relational existence which was incompatible with the uncontrolled exercise of sexuality. To claim this kind of sexual freedom means to violate the limit set by the other person, to exploit, subjugate, enslave, or at least diminish—even if by mutual consent.

The ambiguity of freedom illustrated by this story will emerge more clearly if we recall that the Man who goes beyond the limit is created in the image of God and commissioned to subdue the earth and have dominion. In other words, he is created free like God for a task which he is called upon to fulfil. Some of the implications of this biblical statement for our understanding of freedom are brought out very clearly by Bonhoeffer in his commentary on Genesis 1:26 f.:

> In the language of the Bible, freedom is not something man has for himself but something he has for others. No man is free "as such," that is, in a vacuum, in the way that he may be musical, intelligent or blind as such. Freedom is not a quality of man, nor is it an ability, a capacity, a kind of being that somehow flares up in him. Anyone investigating man to discover freedom finds nothing of it. Why? because freedom is not a quality which can be revealed—it is not a possession, a presence, an object, nor is it a form for existence—but a relationship and nothing else. In truth, freedom is a relationship between two persons. Being free means "being free for the other," because the other has bound me to him. Only in relationship with the other am I free.[2]

If we accept this, we must agree that there can be no freedom *from* without freedom *for,* which will imply that freedom is not something you acquire simply by declaring yourself free or walking out of a prison gate or an attorney's office or the house you were brought up in. It will also give back some of the meaning to the often used (and abused) cliché that there

---

[2]Dietrich Bonhoeffer, *Creation and Fall, Temptation,* trans. J. C. Fletcher (New York: Macmillan, 1965), p. 37.

can be no freedom without responsibility, since freedom will be seen in the first instance as freedom to respond or relate to another person.

The freedom theme runs strongly like a river throughout the early Hebrew tradition, which is probably why biblical imagery has always appealed to oppressed minorities. Exodus from Egypt is a passing from slavery to freedom and an emancipation from bondage to fixed religious myths. The prophets struggle for the freedom of their God against those who wanted to tie him down to certain places, times, and religious dogmas or against the many who wanted a tame God on a string. And since even God's freedom is not for himself but for man, the prophets' struggle is also waged on behalf of human freedom. The prophets' aversion towards the orgiastic and ecstatic cults of Canaan was not dictated by any compulsive fear of a freely expressed instinctual life. They saw these cults as an expression of unfreedom, of man so enslaved to his environment that the undertaking of a genuine life-project was rendered impossible. Man's destiny is to subdue the earth and have dominion, and this is only possible at the price of being free of the world, including the dark; impersonal forces within, which tie man to the earth and threaten to dominate his existence. Against the whole trend of religious thinking at that time, man's ability to achieve this destiny and bring off this freedom is asserted not just by the prophets but throughout the tradition—"Its desire is for you, but you can master it." Paradoxically, the law is also an instrument of freedom precisely by indicating limits within which alone a truly relational existence is possible. For biblical tradition, at least, there need be no opposition between law and freedom.

We need not press too hard the suggestion that what is true theologically is also true psychologically. The corrosion of ecclesiastical and parental authority, together with the religious symbols which have for so long validated such authority, has probably helped give many people, especially young people, the illusion of being free. It may blind them, therefore, to the fact that freedom is a never ending task. Anyone is "free" to remain at the narcissistic level of total self-gratification, but that is not the kind of freedom we are speaking of here.

If we pass on to investigate the possibility of a uniquely Christian understanding of freedom, we could do no better than begin with Paul since his extant correspondence shows a certain interest, we might say obsession, with this theme. The most natural starting point would be his remarkable claim that the Christian is free of the law. He obviously does not mean by this that the Christian is no longer bound by negative commands of the decalogue such as those concerning adultery or murder, nor does he imply that the Christian is free to disregard the civil law. And if we suppose him to mean that the ritual requirements of Jewish law are now obsolete, we have to account for the fact that he puts quite a few laws of his own in their place, some of which are just as irrelevant for us today as the ritual laws were for him. What, then, does he mean by saying that "Christ has redeemed us from the curse of the law" (Gal. 3:13)?

For a Jew, and especially for a Pharisee such as Paul was, Torah observance was *the* means of justification and salvation. He who observed the Torah was assured of acceptance by God. While not denying this possibility in the abstract, Paul maintained that in fact it had not happened, that historically the real function of the law had been "because of transgressions," that is, to show up the reality of culpability and the impossibility of exoneration. This implied the belief that law observance had become a technique of self-exoneration, an unsuccessful attempt to exorcise an inauthentic sense of guilt, a process involving what Heidegger called "forgetfulness of self." The same would be true of ritual practices, and Paul in fact shows the same attitude to these as he does to the law. Consequently, freedom for the Christian would imply release from the need to live on this closed circuit of guilt and exoneration. Before he

could begin to live for God and for others, the Christian had first to die to the law.

This thesis is worked out with remarkable consistency in his letter to the Roman church. After stating the universality of culpability in both Jew and Gentile, he goes on to show that neither had found a way out of the closed circle of sin, guilt, and retribution. The reality of culpability (conversely, the righteousness of God, Romans 3:21) is revealed and the mask penetrated by the accusation of an unfulfilled law, revealing man as sinful, even though he refuses to recognize it. The closed circle is penetrated only from the outside, by the gift of pardon and acceptance offered through Christ. Seen in this light, the death of Jesus has for Paul a twofold purpose: to reveal in all its naked horror the reality of man's real culpability, and, to hold out the offer of pardon and acceptance on condition that he accepts himself as he is. This implies that culpability and forgiveness go far beyond the categories of a written law and at the same time shows up the "boasting" of the "just man" who limits himself to the confines of law observance. To repent is first and last to accept the offer of forgiveness, which implies also acceptance of self in place of the torture and self-hatred of man existing inauthentically under the prohibition. This acceptance brings the peace which Paul describes as "this grace in which we stand" (Rom. 5:2). And since the acceptance takes place in the shared experience of a community, there is also the healing of wounds and the removal of barriers between men, the possibility of freedom for the service of others.

Though it is generally inadvisable to indulge in psychological theorizing on the basis of what has survived of Paul's correspondence, we could be forgiven for detecting a personal note in the way he speaks of the dissolution of a false world of guilt and exoneration. The immediacy of his language has, here and there, something in common with that of a person who has passed through deep therapy. In coming through this *rite de passage,* he evidently has tapped a source of enormous psychic energy which permeates his whole activity and everything he wrote.

The only positive function which Paul ascribes to the law is that of tutor or custodian until such time as guidance was no longer needed (Gal. 3:23-25). The time of the law, therefore, corresponds to the parasitic stage when all the child can do is accept and interiorize the command or prohibition. As often as not, this results in the kind of solitary battle with the instincts described in Romans 7:15-25:

> I do not understand my own actions. For I do not do what I want, but I do the very thing I hate. Now if I do what I do not want, I agree that the law is good. So when it is no longer I that do it, but sin which dwells within me. For I know that nothing good dwells within me, that is, in my flesh. I can will what is right, but I cannot do it. For I do not do the good I want, but the evil I do not want is what I do. . . . Wretched man that I am! Who will deliver me from this body of death?

The "fulness of time" signifies the point at which the child who is also the slave passes from the parasitic stage of false interiority to that of true sonship, a free association with the parent constituted by the mutual calling of names and mutual recognition and acknowledgment. This is the passage from bondage to freedom.

Liberation from law observance as a way of life involves a work of exorcism since "all who rely on works of the law are under a curse" (Gal. 3:10). The exorcism is possible only through the example and the enabling power of Christ, who took the curse upon himself and absorbed it into the freedom of his act. Precisely because he is the prototype of the perfectly free man, he is able to demonstrate and effect this possibility of freedom for others.

The test case for Paul, at least initially, was circumcision. It will be recalled that for Freud circumcision was a ritual substitute for castration carried out by the father on his sons

and therefore bore the marks of that fear of the father which is at the source of the religious neurosis. For Paul (who also, incidentally, speaks of castration in connection with circumcision in Galatians 5:12) the sign of the new freedom is a complete indifference with regard to this practice. It makes no difference one way or the other since "in Christ Jesus neither circumcision nor uncircumcision is of any avail" (Gal. 5:6). That so many of his Christians were hesitant to abandon this practice, or having abandoned it, later came back to it proves how easy it is to revert to the interiorized parental prohibition, a narcissistic interiority which dries up the source from which the new life of freedom for oneself and for others springs.

While on this subject, we do not need to indulge in any facile psychologizing to suspect that the process of identifying with the accusing and forbidding parent operates most strongly and the need to exonerate guilt arises most sharply in the area of sexuality. This is confirmed not only by personal experience but also by the many ritual taboos which surround the exercise of sexuality. Here more than elsewhere, there is felt the need to exorcise the demon and drive the goat into the desert; and here, too, the step must be taken from self-imprisonment in a festering world of guilt to freedom for self and for others. Many of Paul's readers evidently felt they had made this step and that now "all things are lawful" since the prohibition was no longer operative. Against these he points up the paradox that when freedom is interpreted as unlimited sexual gratification, the circuit has not been broken at all, and they are still "under the law"; their freedom is illusory. As another New Testament writer succinctly puts it: "whatever overcomes a man, to that he is enslaved" (2 Pet. 2:19). Freedom has to be maintained at the holding point of tensions pulling in several directions away from genuine personhood and relational existence. While it would be misleading to suggest that Paul was speaking from a perfectly central position as a well-integrated person with no axes of his own to grind (there are some fairly obvious indications to the contrary), he did find it necessary to fight on two fronts: against those who wanted to go back to law observance and against those who took the antinomian view that "all things are lawful." Therefore, we should not make too much of the fact that when he catalogs various vices to be avoided he gives so much space to sexual irregularity. Also, we should have to take account, of course, of the milieu in which his readers found themselves.[3]

We hardly could go much further without having to deal with the accusation, still often heard, that Paul is somehow responsible for the deterrent and negative thinking which has gone into so much of the churches' teaching on sexuality. In the article referred to earlier, for example, Robert Gordis attributes to Paul a view of sex as basically evil, and Simone de Beauvoir makes the surprising statement that Paul perpetuated a savage antifeminism characteristic of Judaism.[4] It may be, as Sherwin Bailey suggests, that Paul was temperamentally averse to marriage; although we should add that it is by no means as certain as generally supposed that he was never married.[5] Here as elsewhere, much confusion has arisen on account of the bad old habit of taking biblical statements out of the context in which they were first made and in which alone they can be understood. It would be naive, for example, to take his injunctions to women to be subject to their husbands, to dress modestly,

---

[3]Relevant passages are: Gal. 5:19; Rom. 1:24-31; 1 Cor. 6:9-10. We should note in this last passage that the Revised Standard Version translation-word "homosexuals" is ambiguous and could be misleading. The two Greek words refer to catamites and pederasts.

[4]Simone de Beauvoir, *The Second Sex*, trans. H. M. Parshley (New York: Knopf, 1953), Bantam Books edition, 1961, p. 90.

[5]In the much-quoted 1 Cor. 7:8, "To the unmarried and the widows I say that it is well for them to remain single as I do" (Revised Standard Version), we should note that the word "single" does not occur in the Greek. We cannot easily exclude the possibility that Paul had married earlier in life and separated from his wife by mutual consent to pursue his mission alone. Parallels for this practice could be found in contemporary Judaism. If we suppose that Paul was a rabbi, or the first century equivalent of one, he would have found it difficult to avoid the duty of marrying when young.

to be silent and submissive, as indicative of antifeminism when they are the kind of injunction we would have expected from any (male) teacher, rabbi, or church leader at that time. To be fair, we also should add that for Paul the cultural and sociological differentiation of the sexes was, at least in principle, superseded in the new community of Christ (Gal. 3:28). If, moreover, he was so antifeminist, how do we explain the numerous friendships he struck up with women and the important part they played in the life of the communities founded by him?

The main bone of contention is, of course, the advice he gives on sexual conduct in reply to queries from members of the Corinthian community (1 Cor. 7). It must cause some surprise that those who think of Paul as antisexual and antifeminist should have so consistently left out of account the determining factor: that the advice is given "in view of the impending disaster" and in the conviction that "the form of this world is about to pass away." We might suppose, to take a distant analogy, that there would be some polarization of ethical attitudes among religious people in California convinced of the prophetic word that that state was about to disappear into the Pacific (they would at least have the advantage over the Corinthians that they could go elsewhere, as some in fact have). A closer and perhaps more useful analogy would be that of the Qumran community, whose attitude to marriage and sexual relations in general was also to a great extent determined by the expectation of an imminent end. If we take due note of this, as we must, we may find that Paul evinces a high level of moral realism and a remarkable freedom of spirit. He takes it for granted that "whoever is firmly established in his heart, being under no necessity but having his desire under control," has all that is needed to come to his own conclusions. He disclaims the intention to put any restraint on his correspondents (1 Cor. 7:35), nor does he do so. All he does is state his own conclusion that, in view of the critical situation, the best course is to remain as one is, though each one is free to take whatever course of action is dictated by his or her particular situation. If the churches had always shown the same realism and the same trust, we would doubtless have been spared much of the confusion and uncertainty which exists today.

The same refusal to broach the freedom of the individual Christian is manifest in those passages where Paul speaks of conscience. Etymologically, both in English and Greek, conscience connotes consciousness, awareness, and making decisions in a truly personal way. As it happens, Paul raises the question of conscience in relation to a subject which has little or no relevance for most people today—that of *kosher* food. What matters, however, is the principle behind the issue:

> If one of the unbelievers invites you to dinner and you are disposed to go, eat whatever is set before you without raising any question on the ground of conscience. (But if some one says to you, "This has been offered in sacrifice," then out of consideration for the man who informed you, and for conscience' sake—I mean his conscience, not yours—do not eat it.) For why should my liberty be determined by another man's scruples? (1 Cor. 10: 27-29).

What seems to lie behind this way of speaking is a conviction of the need to come to responsible decisions which can be translated into action.

The "weak man" (1 Cor. 8:11) is the one who, conscious in a confused way of his newly found freedom, is caught nevertheless halfway; he has not the quality of conviction which carries over into action; and he allows himself to be compromised by the way he sees others behaving. Since freedom can only be exercised in relation to others, Paul insists on due regard for those who are not yet too sure of themselves, which implies a conscious abdication from the full range of options open to the man whose spirit is free and who knows where he stands. Here again, it can be seen how freedom is always correlative with responsibility.

A much more accessible example of the ambiguities of

freedom can be studied in Paul's answer to those who were convinced that there was nothing wrong with casual sexual relations. Readers of Krafft-Ebing, Kinsey, and Vance Packard will know, of course, if they have not already observed it for themselves, that most people who evince a certain casualness (not to say promiscuity) in sexual relations do not feel the need to provide justification for their conduct, not at least at the conscious level. Some, however, do feel this need and occasionally come up with explanations more ingenious than convincing. We may take it that the Corinthian Christians whom Paul is answering were of the latter kind; otherwise, they would hardly have taken the trouble to write. Living in a sleazy city famed throughout the world for its brothels, many of the neo-converts must have found it difficult to break away from former associates and their haunts. Since obviously they could no longer use the cover of "sacred" prostitution (for which Corinth was also famous), they were obliged to take a different line to justify even the occasional visit to a brothel. So we find Paul quoting back at them certain expressions which were common among them: "all things are lawful for me," "food is meant for the belly and the belly for food" (adding as an explanatory gloss that God will destroy both one and the other, so what does it matter?). It seems a trifle pedantic to suppose that this attempt to trivialize sexual relations derived from Gnostic groups of the kind which Paul had to combat elsewhere. Dual-istic ideas of a kind characteristic of the Gnostics were in the air everywhere at that time, and this would not be the first or the only case of *l'homme moyen sensuel* using quasi-philosophi-cal jargon to justify a way of life on which he had already embarked.

We should note that, in dealing with this assumption, Paul does not continue the argument on the rational or naturalistic level. He speaks at once of conclusions which flow necessarily from the new life in Christ; the introductory formula: "surely you know" ("how could you not know?") occurs six times in this chapter alone (1 Cor. 6). "The body is not meant for immorality, but for the Lord, and the Lord for the body" (1 Cor. 6:13). This way of speaking is very strange indeed:

> The body is for the Lord.
> The Lord is for the body.

What can this mean? If we read on a little further, we may find a clue: "Do you not know that your bodies are members of Christ?" (1 Cor. 6:15). This is one of those texts which is so familiar to the church-going Christian that he assumes he knows what it means; and the fact that it is an oratorical question whose answer must be obvious to any intelligent person makes it difficult to answer, "No, I don't!" Yet, how can one's body be part of the body of someone else? A violent and even indecent image!

> Do you not know that your bodies are members of Christ? Shall I therefore take the members of Christ and make them members of a prostitute? Never! Do you not know that he who joins himself to a prostitute is one body with her? For, as it is written, "The two shall become one." But he who is united to the Lord becomes one spirit with him (1 Cor. 6:15-17).

This is an intemperate and almost intolerable way of speaking when we get its import. It is clear that throughout this whole passage the thinking is focused on sexual relations and we are, of course, meant to think of the societal and ecclesial associations which have gathered around this biblical image of sexual union throughout the tradition. In the course of his answer to this particular problem, an answer he addresses to the individual Christian not to the community as a whole, he uses three associative terms of reference: body, sexual partner, temple. The tension and even dislocation in the use of language in this paragraph derive from the transferring of these terms from the collective to the individual since elsewhere he applies all three to the Christian community as a whole. As a result, in

each case the expression is forced and harsh: the body of the individual Christian joined to that of Christ, whereas it is the entire community which forms his body; the image of sexual partnership which cannot be pressed at all, but which is used elsewhere of the church; an individual Christian as temple, whereas throughout the tradition the "church" of Israel is represented as a building and occasionally a temple. This will be seen more clearly if we compare an earlier rhetorical question— "Do you not know that you are God's temple and that God's Spirit dwells in you?" (1 Cor. 3:16)—with the question asked here of the individual Christian—"Do you not know that your body is a temple of the Holy Spirit within you?" (1 Cor. 6:19).

This shows, by the way, that Paul's thinking cannot be followed along a straight logical line; we have to look for the associative links at a deeper level. When, for example, he speaks of Christ as the head of the body we should not press the metaphor too far since he is not thinking anatomically; otherwise, we might end up by speaking of the·Virgin Mary as the neck of the Mystical Body! There are also cases where he juxtaposes different figures, as when he speaks of "building up the body of Christ." What we have to look for is the sense of organicity and dynamic unity, the main thrust of his thinking beneath the changing metaphors.

What basically he is dealing with in this passage is the social and ecclesial implications of the moral activity of the individual Christian. These Corinthians had fastened onto a specious religious argument which seemed to suit their inclinations very well: God will destroy both the food eaten and the one who eats it;[6] the body can have no real religious significance since it is doomed to perish; only the soul matters and that is already committed to Christ in faith. Hence, what does it matter how we seek relief from sexual tension? To this way of thinking, Paul opposes his own understanding of the bodily existence of the Christian. Here we have to bear in mind the semantic prob-

---

[6]Eating is a common euphemism for coition in the Old Testament.

lems involved in the Pauline use of the words "body," "flesh," and "spirit."[7] These are not different parts or ingredients of man but man as a totality seen from different points of view. Man as "flesh" is man in his fallenness, his distance from God; as "body" he is seen in his real, historical existence, still in his fallenness but open to the possibility of transformation; man as "spirit" is man transformed or in the process of transformation. We should further recall that for the biblical tradition in which Paul stands, the body is not, as for the Greeks, the principle of individuation and therefore separation but of solidarity. Man does not exist *in* a body but *as* a body; the body is the essential mode and form of his existence. Hence, Paul would hardly have agreed with the way John Donne speaks of the bodies of the two lovers in *The Extasie*:

> They are ours, but they are not wee, Wee are
> The intelligence, they the spheare.
> We owe them thankes, because they thus,
> Did us, to us, at first convay.

In his answer Paul concentrates on a Christian understanding of bodily existence. Every sin committed by the Christian, no matter how personal and intimate, is directed against the Body of Christ in which he is and therefore against the whole fellowship. In using such phrases as: "the body is meant for the Lord and the Lord for the body," "your bodies are members of Christ," "he who is united with the Lord becomes one spirit with him," he is not saying that you have to choose between casual liaison with a prostitute and union with the Lord since it was obvious to him, as it is to us, that this way of speaking cannot be pressed. If we bear in mind the continuous interaction between the individual and the collective reference of the language used, we may find here an intuition of the societal

---

[7]Pauline anthropology is dealt with briefly and clearly in J. A. T. Robinson, *The Body: A Study in Pauline Theology* (Naperville, Ill.: Allenson, 1957), pp. 17-33.

and relational implications of sexual activity. Even apart from the new being into which the faithful Christian has been taken up, it is impossible to think of sexual activity as the satisfaction of an appetite like eating and drinking ("food is meant for the belly and the belly for food") since this would cancel out the unique freedom of man who, unlike any other animal, can make a free gift of sex. If sex is to be understood in the context of word, language, communication, relational existence, it would follow, as Paul says—though we might word it differently—that "every other sin which a man commits is outside the body; but the immoral man sins against his own body." The evil of casual sex is not just that it trivializes the deepest instinct of man; it also, by implication, frustrates the purpose of bodily existence which is to relate responsibly and creatively to others. For Paul the primacy of bodily existence is sealed by the resurrection of the body—"God raised the Lord, and will also raise us up by his power." Hence, the impossibility for the Christian of considering the body as simply a means to an end:

> The life of the body, like life in general, is both a means to an end and an end in itself. To regard the body exclusively as a means to an end is idealistic but not Christian for a means is discarded as soon as the end is achieved. It is from this point of view that the body is conceived as the prison from which the immortal soul is released for ever by death. According to the Christian doctrine, the body possesses a higher dignity. Man is a bodily being and remains so in eternity as well. Bodiliness and human life belong inseparably together. And thus the bodiliness which is willed by God to be the form of existence of man is entitled to be called an end in itself.[8]

What Paul says and implies in this passage is addressed, of course, to Christians and presupposes only such common ground as is shared by Christians. But it also contains a hard realism which can confront the large-scale trivialization and de-

---

[8]D. Bonhoeffer, *Ethics*, trans. N. Horton Smith (New York: Macmillan, 1965), p. 156.

personalization of sex which flourishes today under the banner of sexual freedom. If only because of the fact that Christian attitudes to the body have played a significant part in producing this state of affairs, the witness of the much-maligned Paul ought to be heard. Elsewhere he enjoins, "do not use your freedom as an opportunity for the flesh, but through love be servants of one another." Freedom, here as elsewhere, is freedom not to dominate and exploit but to serve.

5

THE SILENCE OF
THE GOSPELS

In an article which appeared a few years ago in the *Union Seminary Quarterly Review*, Tom F. Driver raised some awkward questions for traditional theology and Christology under the title "Sexuality and Jesus."[1] His main point was that there seemed to be a touchy spot in what he called "the sexual imagination of the church" concerning the silence of the Gospels on any sexual experience or temptation of Jesus. He raised the question whether this pocket of infection could and should be lanced.

The point is well taken. It would be no exaggeration to say that Christian theology has never, despite enormous efforts, found a satisfactory way of presenting the humanity of Jesus. The great Christological debates and the statements of the early councils used concepts of "person," "nature," "substance," et cetera, in a way which is very difficult if not impossible to appropriate today. The question for us is how, if at all, we can bring to expression the faith experience which went into the credal formulas which we still recite in our liturgies. We may put it a little naively by asking how far we may go in affirming the humanity of Jesus. If we are to be "orthodox," we must go all the way, but going all the way can hardly fail to raise some painful questions. What do we understand by

[1]Reprinted in M. E. Marty and D. G. Peerman, editors, *New Theology No. 3* (New York: Macmillan, 1966), pp. 118-132. The following quotations are taken from this edition.

"humanity"? He was truly Man, but was he a man? If we accept the psychophysical bases of "humanity," may we inquire about his blood group and genes? What, on this understanding, do we make of the fiercely defended dogma that he was conceived virginally? Is the statement in the first Gospel that Mary was "found to be with child of the Holy Spirit" a product of Judeo-Christian midrash with allusion to the virgin-daughter of Zion who brings forth the Messiah? Is it based on a mythological world view which must be thoroughly demythologized in order to grasp its meaning? If it is the *literal* truth of the matter implying the physical virginity of the mother, would it not follow that Jesus was physically haploid, a biological freak? And if it is objected that the male element was supplied miraculously by the Holy Spirit, how then was he different physically from other men? If the final answer is that this is a mystery defying human analysis, we still have the right to ask in what way this Jesus differs from the Christ of Docetus and the Gnostics.

More directly to the point raised by Driver, what we know today about "human nature" and "person" would lead us naturally to ask questions about the sexual component of the human nature of Jesus.

To take an extreme example of the confusion involved, those who accept the authenticity of the Turin shroud—and there are still many—are convinced that it furnishes precise evidence about his physical characteristics. Granted all the difficulties of interpretation involved, may we not, on the basis of evidence much less fragile, inquire about his psychic characteristics? For example, the tradition preserved in the Gospels speaks of the anger, tenderness, and the compassion of Jesus. We know something today about the psychosomatic roots of these emotions, and yet, somehow we feel we ought not to draw the conclusions which would suggest themselves immediately in the case of any other person.

The difficulties involved in even broaching this subject are

formidable. Very few have felt entitled to explore even as far as Driver in his moderately worded and tentative article. Several of those who have done so have experienced a predictably violent reaction. This was true, for example, of the suggestion made by Canon Hugh Montefiore some years ago that Jesus may not have married because he was in some way temperamentally averse to marriage. To assume, as the protestors did, that it was antecedently impossible and unthinkable for Jesus to have married makes it very difficult to ask why not, a question which would certainly help to clarify the issue. The supposition seems to be that, while there is an obvious and unmistakable historical dimension to other aspects of Jesus' mission, there is not and cannot be a historical, much less a psychological, explanation for this.

One result of the failure of Christian theologians to deal convincingly with this problem is that it has passed on by default to others whose point of view is far separated from that of orthodox Christianity. Driver refers, 'for example, to the well-known short story of D. H. Lawrence entitled, "The Man Who Died," in which he represents the Resurrection as the belated sexual awakening of Jesus. As Driver points out, this is not so much blasphemous as heretical not only with regard to the Resurrection but to a Christian understanding of sexuality. For while we may sympathize with the revolt of Lawrence against the sexual hypocrisy and doublethink of the Christian society in which he lived, his own version of sex as a dark and sacred mystery has contributed to our living today "on an empty plane of sexual license and the collapse of human meanings."[2]

Even when not focussed directly on this precise point, the protest of the contemporary artist against the orthodox view of Christian experience has related more or less overtly to it. In a newspaper article several years ago, Kingsley Amis complained that Christianity in general and the Gospels in particular

[2]*Ibid.*, p. 121.

give so little help to people struggling with the frustrations and pain inseparable from sexual experience. The same complaint is found in one of Rilke's letters to his friend Ilse Jahr:

> Why, I ask you, if people want to help us, we who are often so helpless, why do they leave us in the lurch at the roots of all experience? Anyone who assisted us *there* could be confident we would demand nothing more of him. For the assistance he would infuse into us would grow of itself with our life and would become greater and stronger simultaneously with it. And would never go out. Why do they not set us into our deepest mystery?[3]

The same point is made more directly and therefore more controversially by Nikos Kazantzakis in his spiritual autobiography, *Report to Greco:*

> What a relief when the flesh does not embroil itself in spiritual concerns but remains on earth, pure and unsullied. Christianity soiled the union of man and woman by stigmatizing it as a sin. Whereas formerly it was a holy act, a joyous submission to God's will, in the Christian's terror-shaken soul it degenerated into a transgression. Before Christ, sex was a red apple; along came Christ, and a worm entered that apple and began to eat it.[4]

Other people complain that it is so difficult as not to be worth the effort to extract from the Gospels guidance on good ethical behavior in sexual matters, but this is not what we are concerned with here. Given the nature of these compositions, no sensible person expects to find in them precise instructions on such questions as birth control, spacing children, or the treatment of the homosexual. The gravamen we are concerned with is that Jesus is presented as untouched by sexual desire in such a way as to make it too easy to conclude that the Christian God looks unfavorably on human sexuality and sexual activity of any kind.

---

[3] *Selected Letters of R. M. Rilke* (London and New York: Macmillan, 1946), p. 339.

[4] Nikos Kazantzakis, *Report to Greco*, trans. P. A. Bien (New York: Simon & Schuster, 1965), Bantam Books, 1966, pp. 356-7.

Driver quickly disposes of two explanations of the silence of the Gospel tradition on the sexuality of Jesus. The first is that the historical situation in which Jesus lived and in which the Gospels were written ruled this out. We could explain in this way, he says, the absence of any reference to the evils of slavery or other social phenomena but not to something of such central significance as the sexuality of the protagonist. This, however, would be acceptable only if we supposed, which no informed person now does, that the Gospels are biographies of Jesus. And even if they are to some extent and indirectly biographical, which we may reasonably suppose, it would still not be so surprising that little or no reference is made to this matter. The life of the Pythagorean sage Apollonius of Tyana, who was roughly contemporary with Jesus, also contains little or no reference to his sexual experiences or temptations. Modern biblical scholarship would tend to agree that very little historically reliable information has survived about the period of Jesus' life before his emergence as preacher of the kingdom. Hard as it may be to admit it, this implies that we know very little indeed about his life with the exception of the last year or two (some would say the last few months)—and that life was certainly longer than the traditional thirty-three years. Nor would it be necessary to suppose what Driver suggests as another possibility, that information of this kind was screened out by the churches which "traditioned" the material from which the Gospels were formed. The fact is that there was simply no interest, initially at least, in anything outside of the short public ministry leading to Christ's death. If we need confirmation, we should reflect on the fact that Paul, overwhelmed as he was with the reality of Jesus, provides us with absolutely no biographical material.

It should be added that the kind of material we find in the early chapters of Matthew and Luke (the so-called Infancy Gospels) represents a much later and secondary stage. The problems of interpretation which arise in this material are so many that it cannot be used safely as historical source material. It is hardly surprising, if none the less significant, however, that most of the popular beliefs which have contributed to the image of Jesus as entirely removed from sexual experience and temptation rest either on questionable interpretations of these early chapters or on that suspect corpus of pious fiction about Jesus' early years which we find in the apocryphal Gospels. The fact is that we have hardly any reliable information one way or the other about the life of Jesus up to his emergence on the public scene in association with the Baptist, since the first followers of Jesus had no interest in recording such information.

Driver goes on to dispose of a further explanation of the silence of the Gospels. This is what he describes as the "traditional" view that any mention of sexuality in connection with Jesus is antecedently excluded since, being sinless, Jesus could not engage in sexual activity of any kind or even be tempted sexually. He does well to raise the point since it obliges the proponents of this view to answer the question why, if Jesus was tempted to other sins, if he was "one who in every respect has been tempted as we are, yet without sinning" (Heb. 4:15), he could not possibly be tempted to sin sexually. So far no one has provided a satisfactory answer to this question in the framework of traditional theology and Christology. If, as the New Testament states explicitly,[5] Jesus could be tempted at all (the author of *Hebrews* says "in every respect"), we could only conclude that he could not be tempted sexually "if sex itself is held to be no part of the original goodness of created man, if it is made to be the very sign and seal of the Fall."[6] In other words, to exclude the possibility of Jesus being tempted to sin sexually would seem to lead inevitably to the heretical

---

[5] Mt. 4:1; Mk. 1:13; Lk. 4:2; Heb. 2:18; 4:15.
[6] Marty and Peerman. *New Theology No. 3*, p. 127.

view of the Gnostics and Manichees that sexuality is inherently evil and outside the responsibility of the God who is the Father of Jesus Christ.

The Gospels also refer to Jesus being tempted (unless we are to interpret the relevant passages as biblical midrash) but are silent on any sexual temptation and contain not the faintest echo of any sexual experience of Jesus. Driver eventually comes up with the solution that Jesus appears in the Gospels as "the great neutralizer of the religious meaning of sex"; hence the silence is positive and full of meaning. For Jesus, sex was neither a mystical force emanating from the divine world nor a demonic force emanating from Satan. It is simply a fact of life, an area of experience in which it is possible to sin as it is in others. Jesus is not isolated from sexuality, but he refuses to confer on it a religious status and meaning. In this respect he was different from other founders of religious movements, who are generally either champions of sexual rejuvenation or negators of sex.   .

We readily may agree that Jesus did not think of sexuality as a divine, overwhelming force. We saw earlier that in this, as in other respects, he radicalizes the demand contained in the Torah. The incidents of the prostitute who washed his feet and the arraignment of the unfaithful wife show that, while readily forgiving those who had loved in a human way not wisely but too well, he condoned neither prostitution nor marital infidelity. It is also true that Jesus gives no grounds for believing that he thought of sexuality as satanic. As we saw in an earlier chapter, the tempting Snake of the Genesis narrative had already before the time of Jesus been identified with Satan, as it is by the author of Revelation (Rev. 12:9). Satan tempts to unchastity (for example 1 Cor. 7:5) as he does to other sins, but it is only with the Gnostics or those influenced by Gnostic or Manichee ideas that we find the view that sex originated with Satan. The four Gospels, unlike the Gospel of Thomas, were not edited by Gnostics and leave no room for this demonic understanding of sexuality.

In spite of this, we may still doubt whether Driver's explanation is either necessary or adequate. It does not seem to be necessary for the reason stated: that we know practically nothing about Jesus' life apart from the death and Resurrection and such actions and sayings from his short public ministry which the Gospel writers thought useful to preserve. Nor does it seem to be adequate for at least one reason, namely, that it does not take account of the atmosphere of acute eschatological crisis through which Jesus lived and in which the records themselves came into existence.

This last point requires further elaboration. Certain sayings attributed to Jesus have survived which may be considered relevant to the matter under discussion. Almost all of them have been, and continue to be, the source of much misunderstanding. If we begin with the Sermon on the Mount, as Driver does, we shall have to put aside at once the blessing on the pure of heart since this does not refer to chastity. We discussed earlier the saying in which Jesus identified lust as the moral equivalent of adultery (Mt. 5:27-28), but we should now go on to note that it is followed immediately by a severe warning against succumbing to temptation:

> If your right eye causes you to sin, pluck it out and throw it away; it is better that you lose one of your members than that your whole body be thrown into hell. And if your right hand causes you to sin, cut it off and throw it away; it is better that you lose one of your members than that your whole body go into hell (Mt. 5:29-30).

From the context it is clear that this is meant to refer specifically to the eye and the hand as the instruments of lustful intent. As Driver notes, however, the saying occurs in a different context later in the same Gospel (Mt. 18:8-9), where

it appears to depend on the slightly longer form in Mark
9:42-48 dealing with scandal. In the edition of the saying in
the Sermon on the Mount (which is what we might call a
catechetical booklet), the eye is mentioned before the hand
since the previous saying speaks of looking lustfully at a
woman. The editor therefore clearly had sexual sin in mind.
He may even have understood "hand" in the sense in which
that word is often used euphemistically in the Old Testament
for the male sexual organ. But in any case, the connection
is that of the editor not of Jesus himself.

A similar editorial problem clouds the issue in the dispute
about divorce occurring later on in this Gospel (Mt. 19:3-12).
After Jesus reaffirms the primary intention of God in marriage
and excludes the option of divorce "except for unchastity"—
however this is interpreted—the disciples exclaim that in that
case it would be better not to marry at all. Jesus replies that
not all can receive this precept but only those to whom it is
given to do so and there follows at once and without introduc-
tion the saying about eunuchs:

> For there are eunuchs who have been so from birth, and there
> are eunuchs who have been made eunuchs by men, and there are
> eunuchs who have made themselves eunuchs for the sake of the
> kingdom of heaven. He who is able to receive this, let him re-
> ceive it (Mt. 19:12).

Here there are some difficulties which are often passed over
too lightly by the commentators. In the first place, the shocked
reaction of the disciples hardly seems justified by what Jesus
has just said about divorce, if what he said is what we find
here. Moreover, what is this precept which only some specially
gifted or graced can receive? It hardly can be the ruling
about divorce since this was not intended just for "those to
whom it is given," based as it is on creation and the divine
command. However difficult, it was meant for everyone; other-

wise, there would be little point in Jesus' rejoinder to the Pharisees. Then again, the casual link between the exclamation of the disciples and the saying about eunuchs is of the most tenuous kind, and, moreover, Jesus says nothing in either criticism or denial of the statement that "it is not expedient to marry." On the contrary, the intention of the saying about eunuchs would be to corroborate it.

It would not be an indication of undue scepticism to suggest that the editorial arrangement of these several sayings, if not one or other of the sayings themselves, reflects the point of view and intention of the Gospel writer and the church for which he was writing. Most critics would agree that here as elsewhere, Matthew is dependent on Mark, and the parallel passage in Mark (10:2-12) passes immediately from the divorce saying to the blessing of the children, omitting the exclamation of the disciples and the eunuch logion. Caution is therefore in order in taking this whole section as indicative of the attitude of Jesus to the question of marriage and abstention from marriage.

In the context of Judaism at that time, the remarkable thing about the eunuch saying is the addition of a third class, those who had made themselves so for the kingdom of heaven. The first two classes are often referred to in rabbinical writings, and in neither case was marriage excluded. In Old Testament legislation eunuchs were excluded from participation in worship (Deut. 23:1) and, therefore, in a real sense from the community. Interestingly enough, this law was also in force in the Qumran community at some stage of its development and perhaps throughout its existence. In Isaiah 56:4-5, however, we find that eunuchs who keep the covenant are promised an everlasting name. The force of this promise will be realized only if we recall that for most of the Old Testament period the only possibility of overcoming death for the Hebrew was through his children in whom his "name" was perpetuated. It is quite possible that this eschatological promise has in-

fluenced the saying about "eunuchs for the kingdom of heaven," whether or not it was spoken by Jesus. What is at least clear is that the motivation for accepting the celibate life, wherever and however it was practiced at that time, was eschatological.

Before we can speak of motivation some difficulties have to be mentioned even if they are not open to definitive solution. In the first place, we cannot suppose *a priori* that "celibacy" meant the same then as it means for us today. It is commonly assumed, for example, that the Qumran community practiced celibacy in the sense of total sexual abstinence. Against this assumption, however, we have the absence of any reference to it in the Manual of Discipline; the prohibition of sexual relations before the age of twenty in the Damascus Document (which would presuppose that no prohibition existed after that age); and the presence of female skeletons in the Qumran cemetery. This would lead us to suspect that if we are to speak of celibacy in this context it must be of a kind· different· from the celibacy inculcated, for example, in *Sacerdotalis Coelibatus*. We cannot exclude the possibility, both for the Qumran community and some of the first disciples of Jesus, that "celibacy" implied not total sexual abstinence but separation from wife and family. As has been suggested recently, the members of the Qumran community at some stage of its evolution may have been permitted to marry and raise childen during early manhood. If, however, they wished to persevere and go on for full membership in the group, they may have been required to separate from their wives and dedicate themselves totally to the eschatological struggle which loomed ahead.[7] Neither in the eunuch saying nor elsewhere in the Gospels do we find any idealization of the single life as such. What is stressed is that no ties *of any kind* must hold a man back from answering the summons and the demand laid upon him by the

---

[7] This view is defended by Abel Isaksson, *Marriage and Ministry in the New Temple* (Lund, 1965), pp. 45-65.

kingdom of God. This explains the consistent refusal of Jesus to get involved with his own immediate relatives and the reward which he promises those of his disciples who had severed family ties. The Lucan version of these sayings is particularly interesting since it includes not only the usual family relationships but also wife and children:

> If any one comes to me and does not hate his own father and mother and wife and children and brothers and sisters, yes, and even his own life, he cannot be my disciple (Luke 14:26).

> There is no man who has left house or wife or brothers or parents or children, for the sake of the kingdom of God, who will not receive manifold more in this time, and in the age to come eternal life (Luke 18:29-30).

We should note that the latter saying refers to some who *had left* their wives and children, and we have reason to believe that this is precisely what some early Christian apostles and missionaries did "on account of the kingdom of heaven." We cannot be certain, of course, but it would be reasonable to suppose that "eunuch"—perhaps first used disparagingly—refers to those who had made this heroic choice. It is at least clear that the first followers of Jesus were uprooted from family life, though we have Paul's word for it that after the death of Jesus many of them went around accompanied by their wives (1 Cor. 9:5).

Jesus' statement that in the risen life "they neither marry nor are given in marriage, but are like angels in heaven" (Mk. 12:25 and parallels) is sometimes taken as encouraging an "angelic" attitude toward sexual experience. We should note, however, that this comes in the context of a dispute with the Sadducees, who found both the resurrection of the dead and the existence of angels objectionable doctrines. Luke's version of this passage (Lk. 20:34-36) suggests that all Jesus meant was that sexual relations are proper to mortal men but have no part to play after death, and we could hardly grumble at

that. In addition, the reference to angels almost certainly suggests an eschatological cast of thought in view of angelic participation in the projected final struggle of the Qumran community and in the final struggle of Jesus himself before his death (Lk. 22:43).

Misinterpretation of these sayings has produced all sorts of bad conclusions: Gnostic condemnation of sexual relations and procreation; self-mutilation for the sake of the kingdom; "saints" who have left their families to fend for themselves; devout souls who have imposed a "virginal" married life on their spouses. These should be sufficient warning against the danger of overinterpreting the silence of the Gospels in terms of either a sexless Jesus or a Jesus elevated above sexuality or even of Jesus as "the great neutralizer of the religious meaning of sex." The silence can be explained adequately by the nature of the material which has gone into the Gospels, the purposes they were meant to serve, and the overwhelming sense of eschatological crisis in which the Jesus-tradition developed and came to be preserved in writing. *Our* problem in understanding Jesus arises from the fact that this sense of crisis, which can be understood only in the framework of late Jewish apocalyptic thinking, has disappeared forever. It was already in process of dissolution during the period of formation of the Gospel tradition, and there is no lack of indications throughout the New Testament of a painful process of adaptation to a changing perspective. The death of individual Christians, for example, obviously raised a problem in some of the early churches (1 Thess. 4:13-18; 1 Cor. 11:30). In the early subapostolic period, we hear of people hinting that there was not going to be a second coming (2 Pet. 3:3), and various explanations were put forward to explain why "all things have continued as they were from the beginning of creation." The tentative working towards an understanding of space as the sphere of divine and demonic activity (a dominant issue among the Gnostics) may also point in the same direction. It would be no exaggeration to say that this shift in perspective is still the central issue for the Christian today.

The process of readjustment can be followed also on the level of attitudes to moral questions. The eschatological demand is not silenced but we find a more pervasive realism in dealing with concrete situations. Rigorist groups like the Ebionite Christians were more and more separated from the mainstream. In the subapostolic period the remarriage of younger widows is not only tolerated but positively inculcated (1 Tim. 5:14). Only men who have proved themselves good husbands and fathers are to be appointed overseers of Christian communities (1 Tim. 3:2-4). Those who go around discouraging young people from marrying are branded as "liars" and are in bad faith (1 Tim. 4:2-3), and the faithful are warned against those who produce spurious arguments in favor of self-abasement and severity to the body (Col. 2:23). Far from being merely prudential or a falling away from first fervor, this realism is of the creative kind shown by Jesus in his dealings with others. Unrealism in moral matters, especially where sexuality is concerned, leads too easily to illusion and illusion to hypocrisy; and it is hardly necessary to add that the churches have not always taken this lesson to heart.

One positive result which emerges from even a cursory study of these much-interpreted sayings of Jesus is that, while challenging the hearer, they reveal nothing biographical about the speaker. Driver makes a good point against the Jesus portrayed by D. H. Lawrence, Lloyd Douglas, Dorothy L. Sayers, and Ronald Duncan in his poem *Judas,* a Jesus who *really* ate, breathed, suffered, and was tempted like other people, in that it proceeds from a latent Docetism which wants assurance "that the Man was man":

Here we touch upon what is the actual offense created by literature that attempts to "prove" the humanity of Jesus. It is not shocking, to me at least, to imagine Jesus moved to love according to the flesh. I cannot imagine a *human* tenderness, which the

Gospels show to be characteristic of Jesus, that is not fed in
some degree by the springs of passion. The human alternative to
sexual tenderness is not asexual tenderness but sexual fear. Jesus
lived in His body, as other men do. But as He is the Authentic
Man, we are not to be shown a proof of this, neither by Him
on our demand nor by a writer on his behalf.[8]

Jesus' refusal to "prove himself a man," or even to identify
himself unambiguously by means of a title or label, derives
precisely from his authenticity and freedom since, as Driver
says, to prove oneself requires to deliver over to another
person the power to judge one's nature. In other words, the
need to prove oneself is symptomatic not of freedom but of
fear. In this respect, the silence of the Gospels on any sexual
temptation or experience of Jesus and the so-called messianic
silence may be mutually illuminating.

The impression of a man so free that he does not have to
prove himself comes through clearly in the longer account of
the temptations to which Jesus was subjected at the outset of
his ministry. These temptations are to deviate from a mission
revealed to him in the experience accompanying his baptism;
the same Spirit which came on him then drove him into the
desert, and Satan's opening gambit—"*if* you are the Son of
God"—attempts to probe into the open the consciousness of
divine sonship which came to him as he stepped out of the
water. Jesus refuses the temptation to appease his hunger miraculously, to throw himself from the top of the temple in
order to compel God, by a spectacular intervention, to con-
firm his sense of mission, and above all he refuses the offer
of political messiahship as he looks out over the land occupied
by the Roman legions. He is here portrayed as a man who
has already found himself, who is free of compulsion and
therefore open to the call which has been addressed to him.

One of the many artists in recent years who have not been
willing to leave it at that is the Cretan writer Nikos Kazant-

[8]Marty and Peerman, *New Theology No. 3*, p. 127.

zakis whose novel, *The Last Temptation of Christ,* is surely the most interesting of the antidocetist protests against the dehumanized Christ of traditional theology. His avowed purpose was to free Christ from the stultifying categories of the theologians and priests so that he could be seen as he was, a model for the man who struggles to go beyond himself, overcome temptation, and achieve union and reconciliation with God. As he tells us in the Prologue, the book is not a biography but the confession of every man who struggles. His object in writing was "that every free man . . . will more than ever before, better than ever before, love Christ."[9] In spite of this, he was rewarded for his pains by virtual excommunication by his church and the refusal of Christian burial in Athens. His book was also placed on the Roman Catholic Index.

Many influences, important in the life of Kazantzakis, converged in this prototype of the truly free man. There is something here of the Nietzschean hero who struggles to assert his life-value against the encompassing fear of death and meaninglessness, something, perhaps, of his heroic if somewhat mythological Cretan ancestors, a great deal of his own passion to express and overcome the dualities he experienced within himself. To speak of dualities opens up for him a new way through the Christological dogma:

> This dual nature of Christ has always been a deep inscrutable mystery to me, and especially the yearning, so human, so superhuman, of Christ the man to attain to God, or, more exactly, to return to God and become identical with Him. This nostalgia, at once so mystical and so real, had opened large wounds in me and also abundant wellsprings . . . . Every man is half God, half man; he is both spirit and flesh. That is why the mystery of Christ is not simply a mystery for a particular creed; it is universal. The struggle between God and man breaks out in everyone, together with the longing for reconciliation. Most often this struggle is unconscious and short-lived. A weak soul does not have the en-

[9]Nikos Kazantzakis, *The Last Temptation of Christ,* trans. P. A. Bien (New York: Simon & Schuster, 1966), p. 4.

durance to resist the flesh for very long. It grows heavy, becomes flesh itself, and the contest ends. But among responsible men who keep their eyes riveted day and night upon the Supreme Duty, the conflict between flesh and spirit breaks out merciless and may last until death.[10]

In keeping with this insight, the evangelical temptations are drastically rewritten. The Christ of Kazantzakis is tempted to pride and participation in violent revolution but also and especially by the sexual instinct. He is torn between a destiny thrust upon him which, however, he comes to accept, and the desire to marry and raise a family, in other words, to be a man like other men. At the age of three, he experienced sexual pleasure with his cousin Mary, one year his senior (this is a copy of an incident which Kazantzakis records of his own childhood), and went through all the emotional and sexual turmoil of adolescence. Newly come to manhood, he went to Cana at his mother's instigation to find a bride for himself, chose Mary, but at the moment of approaching her felt the claws of the murderous divine vulture sinking into his scalp. From that moment he knew he could not escape his destiny, and it was this conviction which drove Mary the Magdalene to a life of prostitution. Tracking him throughout his painful ascent to Golgotha—which lasted all his life—was "the savage body of a woman covered head to foot with interlocking scales of thick bronze armor"[11]—a combination of the Magdalene figure (Woman the Temptress) and the fierce vulture (Yahweh) who drove him on. At the final hour, in the pain and delirium of the Crucifixion, he was subjected to a last temptation by the vision of himself enjoying a happy family life in old age; but he shook his head, cast off the Tempter's vision of despair, and knew that he had not succumbed and that, nailed to the cross, he had reached the summit of sacrifice.

Kazantzakis was perfectly aware, as he stated in the Prologue,

[10]Kazantzakis, *Report to Greco,* p. 277.
[11]Kazantzakis, *The Last Temptation of Christ,* p. 79.

that this was an archetypal rather than a historical figure, the kind of man who can be a model for the heroic struggler, the kind of man, in fact, whom Kazantzakis wished to become (if fitfully) throughout his own painful life. He had his own views on what the churches and priests had made of Christ—the life-denier who glared furiously at him from the icon as he made love to the Irish girl in the chapel, the Crucified who could not be permitted to look on when the monk of Mount Athos found joy for the first time in the arms of a woman. Christ, he felt, had found no hospitality in the Christian churches. He "wanders about hungry and homeless; He is in danger, and it is now his turn to be saved—by man." Obsessed from his earliest years by the mysteriously attraction of the figure behind the icon, he felt that "He . . . was the one lying still dead in my entrails, the one who kept weeping. He was struggling to rise, but could not without man's help, and on account of this he felt great resentment toward me. How was I to save him—and be saved?"[12]

That this figure is so much the antithesis of the hieratic Christ of Greek Orthodox icon-worship, the *pantocrator* who goes to the cross dressed in Byzantine vestments without pain or humiliation, is explained by Kazantzakis' own experience of Christianity. The Christ of Orthodox worship appears in his eternal essence only with his glorification. Following on Johannine theology, particularly influential in the East, the Crucifixion is not a self-emptying but an elevation; and even on the cross the light shines so dazzlingly from within that the beholder does not see the body. Kazantzakis believed that this view of Christ dissolved the tension between soul and body. He could only be presented persuasively, compellingly, if this tension is taken into account. In fact, it is the struggle which this tension generated which lies at the heart of the human mystery of Christ. If the body and the flesh of Christ are not taken with absolute seriousness, there can be no temptation,

[12]Kazantzakis, *Report to Greco*, p. 228.

no struggle, no relevance for the man whose manhood is discovered and defined in terms of struggle. Christianity has lost the sense of the seriousness of bodily existence and must recover it under pain of becoming completely irrelevant.

This was the message left with him by Father Joachim during his visit to the Monastery of Mount Sinai:

> . . . and then the religion of Christ will take another step forward on earth. It will embrace the whole man, all of him, not just half as it does now in embracing only the soul. Christ's mercy will broaden. It will embrace and sanctify the body as well as the soul; it will see—and preach—that they are not enemies, but fellow workers. Whereas now, what happens? If we sell ourselves to the devil, he urges us to deny the soul; if we sell ourselves to God, he urges us to deny the body. When will Christ's heart grow sufficiently broad to commiserate not only the soul but also the body, and to reconcile these two savage beasts?[13]

For Kazantzakis the tension between soul and body, spirit and flesh, is the essence of humanity; hence, the impossibility of affirming the humanity and contemporaneity of Christ without making this tension central to an understanding of his life and mission.

It may seem blasphemous, or at least a caricature, for anyone to project his own life-experience, in particular his sexual experience, onto the figure of Christ. Yet, we repeat, Kazantzakis did not intend to write a biography. When he prevented Joseph from living with Mary as husband with wife by having him struck by a thunderbolt, he was under no illusion even that this might have happened. His book is the outcome of his need to find meaning and genuine contemporaneity. For him, to say that Jesus is divine is to discover in him the embodiment of the truth that man can be more than man, that he can transcend himself and become one with God. To speak of him suffering from those sexual frustrations which are inseparable from the experience of most men is to attempt to say something

[13]*Ibid.*, p. 290.

about the redemptive possibilities of sexual experience and, at the same time, to affirm that the instinctual life can be "transubstantiated" (a favorite term of his) even when it is denied its full expression. There runs throughout the work of Kazantzakis an uneasy tension between the affirmation and denial of sexuality. On the one hand, he comes close to Lawrence when he speaks (not in this book) of Christ being resurrected by the ardent longing of the repentant prostitute and when he refers, as he does often, to the redemptive power of what most people would consider sexual sin. Over against this is an acute sense of a deep-seated hostility between the sexes and, more disturbing, a suspicion that woman incarnates "the adverse powers" (a phrase used in one of his letters) which hold man back from fulfilling his destiny. The ascetic note which runs strongly throughout his own life and that of his Christ is strong enough to leave its mark on the body. In his own case, it had the remarkable effect of disfiguring his whole face with a horrible skin disease during a stay in Vienna, when on impulse he made an assignment with a lady he met by chance. The same fate befell the Christ-figure, Manolios, under similar circumstances in *The Greek Passion*, and he evidently intends us to understand the vulture's claws in much the same way. The marks which they left were just as real as the marks of the nails and the spear.

All of this might seem to lead to the conclusion that the Christ of Kazantzakis was a sexual misfit burdened with complexes. Yet, to draw this conclusion would mean forgetting that without the mission—the task placed upon him—there would be no tension, and that the task is that of everyone who wishes to follow Christ. Only at the price of overcoming temptation does he become "the man for others" or, as Kazantzakis would say, "the great opener." In one of his letters, he asks why Christ exercised such a power of attraction. He answers the question himself: "Because his body had opened up, and his soul inclined towards all human bodies, like the key-bearer,

and he tried to open them with persistence, violence and the ultimate in sweetness"[14] Having found himself at the cost of a hard struggle, Jesus moves among men sunk in the hell of non-recognition and there performs his mission. To say that people are evaluated—*judged*—by their response to this encounter is certainly an orthodox way of putting it and is, in fact, one of the key insights of the Gospel of John.

With all its defects, *The Last Temptation of Christ* is very much more significant for the Christian reader than the many attempts which have been made over the last two centuries, and continue to be made, to represent Christ as an Essene priest, a Zealot, a field preacher in search of a revolution, or a dreamy, unrealistic mystagogue. It should be read not as another attempt to reinterpret Jesus by breaking his mysterious incognito but as the response of a highly sensitive artist and religious thinker to the challenge of his life and death. It makes us ask the question: Do we force Christ inside the dogmas, or do we search for language arising out of our own experience to express the insights which brought the dogmas into existence in the first place? Jesus can be contemporary to us not as a divine essence disguised in human form but by indicating, through the manner of his own living and dying, the ultimacy in our own lives. It is only in this way that *any* speaking about Jesus, including what we find in the Gospels, can have significance and contemporaneity.

---

[14]Helen Kazantzakis, *Nikos Kazantzakis. A Biography based on his Letters,* trans. Amy Mims (New York: Simon & Schuster, 1968), p. 85.

CELEBRATION

One of the main reasons for the widespread dissatisfaction with the churches' attitude to sexuality is the fact that they have almost invariably understood sex as a means to an end rather than an end in itself. In other words, they have spoken much more of the procreative than the creative possibilities of the man-woman relationship. We argued in an earlier chapter that this failure to come to terms with sexuality as such, as opposed to a set of ethical norms or a theology of marriage, has contributed to the isolation and depersonalization of sexuality in our culture. Despite appearances to the contrary, the biologism of some official Roman Catholic pronouncements on the subject and the "sex as fun" thesis have something important in common.

To speak of sexuality as an end in itself obviously requires explanation. Those who subscribe to the "sex as fun" thesis or who, like Alex Comfort, regard it as the most important human sport, also think of it in some way as an end in itself. The trouble is that when sex becomes fun and nothing else, it generally ceases to be fun; the playmate becomes a plaything; the element of lightness and joy goes out of it; it becomes sick. Despite this, there is a sense in which we can and should affirm that sex is fun. *Eros* and fun are closely allied in that both spring from the sense of joy which is spoilt by any thought of purpose. In a way, both are forms of contemplation and have much in common with the dance. Dancing may have been functional in the early stages of human evolution and still today in culturally primitive societies. But to dance is first and fore-

most to "let go" of oneself, to express an inarticulate *Lebens-freude* which carries beyond words. Sexual activity is also functional; but to regard it as *merely* functional is to miss what is unique in man. Only man can laugh, dance, and make love.

The dance is perhaps the most spontaneous and universal symbol of celebration. To dance one must leave the calculating mind and go out of oneself, acquire some capacity for release and ecstasy. Dancing is possible only when we "let go," "go beyond." What Shakespeare said about the man who has no music in his soul can also be said of the man who cannot or will not dance. Dancing begins where words leave off. We recall that Zorba of the famous novel and film asked his learned friend to dance what he had been saying in order that he (Zorba) might understand it. In *Report to Greco* the Muslim dervish at Knossos explains why he dances: "If a man cannot dance, he cannot pray. Angels have mouths but lack power of speech. They speak to God by dancing."[1] Dancing is an extension of the communication effected by words, but further along the spectrum. It is also a reconciliation of warring elements. The Sufi dervishes have always danced with one hand pointing upwards and the other downwards to signify the mystical union and reconciliation between heaven and earth. When they dance, men and women go out of the well-guarded fortress of their own identity and are taken up, however briefly, into a greater and deeper rhythm than that of their everyday lives.[2]

The widely held idea that dancing originated as a device for attracting a prospective sexual partner is probably wrong, even though the sexual implications of dancing are obvious enough and have been given more than their due share of emphasis in the Christian tradition. In a positive sense, however, sexuality has in common with the dance the need for expansion and

---

[1]Kazantzakis, *Report to Greco*, p. 143.
[2]This may be true in a very attenuated form in highly conventionalized "social" dancing, but we are not thinking primarily of this.

self-transcendence. Both are forms of communication beyond the reach of words, and both contain, more or less implicitly, the element of union and reconciliation between opposites. For their performance both demand that the participants go beyond themselves and leave behind the calculating mind.

In view of the parallelism suggested here, it is not surprising that attitudes to dancing prevalent throughout historical Christianity should have paralleled attitudes to sexuality. Preachers have thundered from innumerable pulpits of the dangers of dancing, and quite a dossier of ecclesiastical legislation forbidding either sacred or profane dancing could be compiled without undue difficulty. For our forbears, whether Puritan or Catholic or whatever, dancing was generally considered if not actually sinful at least a proximate occasion of sin. The Christian devil was endowed with many of the characteristics of the baals of Canaan or of Pan and Dionysus, all of whom seem to have been very partial to dancing. We have inherited these devils, and, as the poet says, "it's hard to dance with the devil on your back." Justification for this deterrent note appeared to be available in the Scriptures. Texts could be quoted in favor of the view that dancing is a pagan activity out of keeping with the sobriety which must distinguish a Christian man or woman. But since texts could be quoted which appeared to favor the view that sex was also a pagan activity unbecoming to the Christian, this kind of appeal to the Scriptures inevitably came under suspicion. Hence, it may still not be too late to inquire as to what attitude really prevails in scriptural tradition.

If we start out with attitudes to dancing as a test case for the whole range of possibilities of life-celebration, we come up against the initial difficulty that we encounter the people of Israel only after their life-style had been more or less deeply influenced by that of the peoples among whom they settled. The dance around the bull at the apostate shrine of Bethel (Ex. 32:19) and the wild dance of David before the Ark (2 Sam.

6:14-16) show how deeply Canaanite influence had penetrated and why a certain ambiguity lingered around this kind of dancing. Yet, dancing became an essential element in Hebrew festivals, especially in those involving processions.[3] This was particularly the case at *Sukkoth* (the Feast of Tents) and continued so right down to New Testament times, when a torch dance was performed in the Court of the Women. Even elderly rabbis did not disdain to take part in this dance, and it was said that anyone who had not witnessed the joy on this occasion had never witnessed joy at all. It was implicit in the nature of the Jewish festivals that the dance should symbolize the joy of the kingdom, the same joy which the morning stars and the sons of God celebrated at the creation (Job 38:7). Hence, the pervasive metaphors of the marriage feast, the joy of table fellowship, the drinking of new wine in the kingdom. One holy man, Rabbi Eleazar, even stated that the day would come when the Holy One (blessed be he!) would himself dance in the presence of the righteous. Even Nietzsche could have believed in such a god!

Given, however, that the Old Testament is a prophetic collection and that the writings of the prophets form its most important and characteristic element, we would still have a grave difficulty. The reader who turns from Plato's *Symposium* with its impassioned discussion of *eros* and its celebration of beauty to the Hebrew prophets is at once aware of a tremendous contrast, an unbridgeable chasm. Here, too, there is passion, but with what a difference! Amos, it has been said, moves among men who are condemned to death and do not know it. His words are a counterpoint of doom and condemnation to the carefree celebration of his contemporaries. His god refuses to listen to the melody of harps and demands that the "idle songs" be hushed. As if the hot ash were already falling on the

---

[3] The Hebrew word for feast (*hag*) may, like the Arabic *hadj*, have originally connoted dancing.

doomed city, Jeremiah is commanded to remain wifeless and childless, to absent himself from the great mysteries of birth, marriage, and death and to take no part in their celebration:

> Do not enter the house of mourning, or go to lament, or bemoan them; for I have taken away my peace from this people, says the Lord. . . . You shall not go into the house of feasting to sit with them, to eat and drink. . . . Behold, I will make to cease from this place, before your eyes and in your days, the voice of mirth and the voice of gladness, the voice of the bridegroom and the voice of the bride (Jeremiah 16:5,8-9).

The quality and import of this way of speaking emerges clearly only when we contrast it with the great statements of philosophers and religious thinkers like Plato. With sure insight Heschel develops this point in his opening statement on the prophetic message:

> A student of philosophy who turns from the discourses of the great metaphysicians to the orations of the prophets may feel as if he were going from the realm of the sublime to an area of trivialities. Instead of dealing with the timeless issues of being and becoming, of matter and form, of definitions and demonstrations, he is thrown into orations about widows and orphans, about the corruption of judges and affairs of the market place. Instead of showing us a way through the elegant mansions of the mind, the prophets take us to the slums. The world is a proud place, full of beauty, but the prophets are scandalized, and rave as if the whole world were a slum. They make much ado about paltry things, lavishing excessive language upon trifling subjects. What if somewhere in ancient Palestine poor people have not been treated properly by the rich? So what if some old women found pleasure and edification in worshiping "the Queen of Heaven"? Why such immoderate excitement? Why such intense indignation?[4]

For the prophets there is no time left for celebrating. A whole people lies dying and there is time only to shout the

---

[4]Abraham J. Heschel, *The Prophets* (New York: Harper & Row, 1962), p. 3.

few words which may bring them back to life. For the prophets the question is whether there is time to dance in a burning city. They are no more life-denying than a doctor who is trying to save a dying man. Their condemnation of the present is not that of a bitter critic out of sympathy with his times. On the contrary, it is the only way which they see of opening the future. For, despite the condemnation, the promise still remains and can be heard clearly throughout the doomed land: ". . . there shall be heard again the voice of mirth and the voice of gladness, the voice of the bridegroom and the voice of the bride, the voices of those who sing . . ." (Jer. 33:10-11). As the wisdom-teacher of a later age will say, ". . . there is . . . a time to weep, and a time to laugh; a time to mourn, and a time to dance, . . . a time to embrace and a time to refrain from embracing" (Eccles. 3:1-5).

A similar obstacle awaits us when we turn to those writings in the Old Testament which emanate from the priestly and scribal classes of the postexilic period. What can we expect from this source except jejune scholasticism, all sorts and varieties of sexual and ritual taboos, and a legalism which kills the living spirit of man? Before passing on, however, we should note that the clearest affirmation of the goodness of creation is to be found in the great Creation Hymn in Genesis 1 which comes precisely from this suspect source. It is not just accidental that the writer repeats at each stage the affirmation that everything that God made was good. In view of the well-known similarities between this chapter and the Babylonian creation-poem, *Enuma Elish,* it must be read as a refutation of Babylonian pessimism with regard to the created order and, in particular, to man's place in it. Man is not a puppet set on the stage of the world to relieve the lesser gods of the many chores inseparable from the service of the high gods. On the contrary, what other nations thought of as divine powers—the heavenly bodies and the monsters of the deep—are at his service. Himself in the divine image, he is free of servitude.

able to take his destiny in his own hands—an idea which was quite foreign to religious thinking elsewhere at that time.

That the image and likeness of God is to be located in man's "higher faculties" is an idea proposed by Augustine in his monumental work on the Trinity but which finds no support in the biblical text. The theophany described by the priest Ezekiel appears in the likeness "as it were of a human form" (Ezek. 1:26). Conversely, man reflects the divine being in the form of existence which is proper to him, namely, as a body and, more specifically, as a sexual being, since "man" is created male and female. It is in the flesh that man is to celebrate his freedom and "sing for joy to the living God" (Ps. 84:2) with all the chorus of creation.

We find a different situation again when we turn to the wisdom-teachers for enlightenment or for encouragement in celebrating the joys of bodily existence. Much of the material that we find in Proverbs, composed for the most part of collections of maxims, has a practical, eudaimonistic, and even prudential ring about it. In its demand for sanity and respect for limits, it must seem to us today to be decidedly middle-class, though in this as other respects it follows fairly closely the ideal of the good life elaborated by sages throughout the ancient Near East from the earliest times. The ideal is the "cool" man—he who restrains his words and has a cool spirit (Prov. 17:27). Wisdom means conforming to the law of the cosmos embodied in the social order and certain ethical norms. Not surprisingly, therefore, the wisdom-teachers extol the sober pleasures of family life—"a good wife is the crown of her husband," "a prudent wife is from the Lord"—and warn repeatedly against the danger of the unattached woman. Within this model, according to which everything must be done "decently and in order," there seems to be little room for the expansive possibilities of human life and celebrating the joys of the body.

Appeals to live by order can be successful over a long period of time, but sooner or later embarrassing questions begin

to be asked, the forces kept at bay begin to press against the perimeter of defense, and the cool man "loses his cool." The conflict between traditional wisdom and personal experience is a recurrent phenomenon: it emerged in ancient Egypt in the so-called Dispute about Suicide and the Protest of the Eloquent Peasant; in ancient Mesopotamia in various dialogues which take a detached and cynical view of the received wisdom,[5] and it is very much in evidence today. In the Old Testament both Job and Qoheleth break away from the wisdom tradition to which they belong in their stubborn refusal to accept easy solutions or value systems which appear to conflict with the immediate data of experience. The latter in particular forces his audience to face facts and question the received doctrines: Is it true that virtue is always rewarded; that the possession of wisdom, knowledge, and riches makes a man happy; that we must sit quietly under injustice in the certainty that the oppressor will come to a bad end? In particular, he forces them to face the certainty of death; in fact, what he appears to be saying is that death is the *only* certainty and that the only advantage the living have over the dead is that the former know that they will die, while the latter do not know anything. This may seem to lead to a pessimistic and even cynical attitude to life, but what is remarkable in Qoheleth is his strong affirmation of the value of life and the right to bodily life in the face of and even because of the certainty of death:

He who is joined with all the living has hope, for a living dog is better than a dead lion. For the living know that they will die, but the dead know nothing . . . . Go, eat your bread with enjoyment, and drink your wine with a merry heart; for God has already approved what you do. Let your garments always be white; let not oil be lacking on your head. Enjoy life with the wife whom you love, all the days of your vain life which he has given you under the sun, because that is your portion in life and

[5]See James B. Pritchard, ed., *Ancient Near Eastern Texts Relating to the Old Testament,* 2d ed. (Princeton, N. J.: Princeton University Press, 1955), pp. 405-10.

in your toil at which you toil under the sun. Whatever your hand finds to do, do it with all your might; for there is no work or thought or knowledge or wisdom in Sheol, to which you are going (Eccles. 9:4-10).

We should not minimize the significance of this ethical realism. It is only too easy for the Christian reading the New Testament to suppose somehow that he is already *there* or to use the Christian hope as an escape chute away from the realities, both ecstatic and painful, of personal experience. If one lives in the belief that one's destiny is to be a disembodied spirit for all eternity, then the thing to do would be to live as "spiritually" as possible. In that case, it would be difficult to see what place there could be for celebrating the joys of bodily existence. Qoheleth's death-oriented ethic acts as a strong acid upon the illusions which so easily build up around Christian hope. Only the man who knows that he will die knows what life means; only he who has tasted this bitter certainty can eat of the fruit of life and enjoy its savor.

It hardly needs to be said that life does not always take on the same color in the light of this certainty. The quality of life-affirmation of Camus' rebel is very different, for example, from that of the Dionysian protagonist in *Zorba The Greek*. The wisdom-tradition of Israel was also conscious of the ambiguities involved in affirming the reality and certainty of death. One reaction, perhaps the most common, would be a despairing hedonism which is really a denial of life. The author of *The Wisdom of Solomon,* writing probably in Alexandria shortly before the time of Christ, puts this into the mouth of the Jewish apostate who has fallen under the allure of Epicurean philosophy:

"Short and sorrowful is our life,
and there is no remedy when a man comes to his end,
and no one has been known to return from Hades.
Because we were born by mere chance,
and hereafter we shall be as though we had never been;

because the breath in our nostrils is smoke,
and reason is a spark kindled by the beating of our hearts.
When it is extinguished, the body will turn to ashes,
and the spirit will dissolve like empty air.
Our name will be forgotten in time,
and no one will remember our works;
our life will pass away like the traces of a cloud,
and be scattered like mist
that is chased by the rays of the sun
and overcome by its heat.
For our allotted time is the passing of a shadow,
and there is no return from our death,
because it is sealed up and no one turns back.

"Come, therefore, let us enjoy the good things that exist,
and make use of the creation to the full as in youth.
Let us take our fill of costly wine and perfumes,
and let no flower of spring pass by us.
Let us crown ourselves with rosebuds before they wither.
Let none of us fail to share in our revelry,
everywhere let us leave signs of enjoyment,   ,
because this is our portion, and this is our lot" (Wis. 2:1-9).

Despite the semblance of similarity, there is a world of difference between this kind of life-affirmation and what we read in Qoheleth:

There is nothing better for a man than that he should eat and drink, and find enjoyment in his toil (Eccles. 2:24).

I know that there is nothing better for them than to be happy and enjoy themselves as long as they live; also that it is God's gift to man that every one should eat and drink and take pleasure in all his toil (Eccles. 3:12-13).

Behold, what I have seen to be good and to be fitting is to eat and drink and find enjoyment in all the toil with which one toils under the sun the few days of his life which God has given him, for this is his lot (Eccles. 5:18).

I commend enjoyment, for man has no good thing under the sun but to eat and drink, and enjoy himself, for this will go with him in his toil through the days of life which God gives him under the sun (Eccles. 8:15).

There is a "letting go" in Qoheleth but of a very different kind from that of the apostate Jew. He tells us to cast our bread upon the waters and to live and work strongly even though all will end in death—"whatever your hand finds to do, do it with all your might; for there is no work or thought or knowledge or wisdom in Sheol, to which you are going" (Eccles. 9:10).

The difference is in the quality of the affirmation. Coming to terms with death must not lead to despair or a frantic immersion in pleasure which would in any case imply that one had not come to terms at all. Paradoxically, it can lead to a great sense of release and unburdening, a slackening of that terminal anxiety which colors all the activity of the person whose life is governed at every point by the attempt to forget death. The passages quoted above are really an exhortation to put aside vain anxiety, to accept and learn to live with what you cannot change, to learn to *be what you are*—all of which is not so far removed from the wisdom inculcated by Jesus:

> Do not be anxious about your life, what you shall eat or what you shall drink, nor about your body, what you shall put on. Is not life more than food, and the body more than clothing? Look at the birds of the air: they neither sow nor reap nor gather into barns, and yet your heavenly Father feeds them. Are you not of more value than they? And which of you by being anxious can add one cubit to his span of life? And why are you anxious about clothing? Consider the lilies of the field, how they grow; they neither toil nor spin; yet I tell you, even Solomon in all his glory was not arrayed like one of these . . . . Therefore do not be anxious, saying, 'What shall we eat?' or 'What shall we drink?' or 'What shall we wear?' For the Gentiles seek all these things; and your heavenly Father knows that you need them all (Mt. 6: 25-32).

It may be too much to say that Qoheleth has discovered

the paradox that only the person who acknowledges death can celebrate life, but he has stated it with a clarity unequalled elsewhere in the tradition. We can estimate its value for us today if we compare it with some allegedly Christian forms of life-denial, or with the still prevalent "romantic" view of love, or with the Freudian interpretation of life as a roundabout way to death; above all, if we take stock of the death-anxiety which plays such a determining role in our own culture. It is, to be sure, not the last word, certainly not for the one who looks to Christ and celebrates his dying into new life. But it remains one which is too important for us to forget.

If we go on to speak of celebrating the creative possibilities of the man-woman relationship, we have the initial disadvantage in the tradition that all the prophets, priests, and wisdom-teachers were, without exception, men. It is not surprising, therefore, to find a certain note of reserve in the way the various writers speak of women. David, to be sure, was guilty of adultery and thereby merited death, but there is more than a hint that Bathsheba lured him on and cooperated, at least by her silence, in the cold-blooded murder of her husband.[6] The career of Solomon admirably illustrated the warning of a later wisdom-teacher,

Give not your strength to women,
Your ways to those who destroy kings (Prov. 31:3),[7]

since it was his addiction to the joys of the harem which was the occasion, if not the direct cause, of his fall from grace. The danger *to man* of the footloose woman away from her husband is thematic in the first collection contained in the Book of

[6]Legitimately we may ask why she chose to bathe on the roof of a house from which she was visible to the palace, and her message to David seems more like a cry of triumph than a signal of distress.

[7]We now know from the Ugaritic texts that the Hebrew word translated "ways" in Revised Standard Version can also mean "virility." R. B. Y. Scott, ed. *Proverbs and Ecclesiastes* (New York: Doubleday, 1965), p. 183, emends to the Hebrew word for "loins" but this does not seem necessary.

Proverbs (chapters 1-9). In the sagas of the Patriarchs, woman stands out as a negative figure of contrast, though no criticism is voiced when Abraham (or was it Isaac?) endangered the "virtue" of his wife in order to save his own skin or when Lot threw his daughters out to the sex-crazed mob at Sodom. At regular intervals throughout Proverbs, we come upon sour comments on the fragility and worse of womankind—

It is better to live in a corner of the housetop
than in a house shared with a contentious woman.

It is better to live in a desert land
than with a contentious and fretful woman.

A continual dripping on a rainy day
and a contentious woman are alike.

These may be of no more universal significance than the statement of one of Shakespeare's characters that "war is no strife to the dark house and the detested wife," but the fact remains that men also can be contentious, fretful and in general objectionable to women, though little allusion is made to this possibility in the biblical tradition. The fact is that only rarely do the wisdom writers go beyond the practical aspects of every-day living and pause to wonder at the mystery of the man-woman relationship ("the way of a man with a maiden," Prov. 30:19). They were men, they wrote for men, and their outlook on life was severely conditioned by the sociological and cultural realities of their age.

It has been noted more than once in previous chapters how mainstream Western Christianity so often has absorbed nega-tive and deterrent elements in the Old Testament to the neglect of the prophetic and creative insights, the points at which the biblical writers go beyond the time-conditioned milieu in which they lived. The reediting which Jerome carried out in his translation of *Esther, Judith,* and *Tobit* are well known, as are

some tendentious interpretations of key texts by Augustine.[8] Rather than go over once again this well-worn terrain, it would serve our purpose better at this point to take another look at what is surely the most surprising composition in the scriptural canon, the Song of Solomon.

One of the greatest paradoxes of the Jewish faith is that it could accomodate such violent contrasts as the prophets of doom and the sensuous beauty of Solomon's most excellent canticle. Both Jewish and Christian theologians have tried to dissolve the scandal of uninhibited *eros* contained in the Canticle. Though the great rabbi Akiba declared that "all the ages are not worth the day on which the Song of Songs was given to Israel," he also cursed those who gave it a literal interpretation. The exegesis of the Canticle throughout the Christian tradition provides by itself an explanation of the present impasse with regard to erotic experience. Not that the allegorical interpretation was wrong in itself. In view of the prophetic insights of Hosea, it was, on the contrary, inevitable and proved profoundly meaningful. What was misleading was the allegorical interpretation to the exclusion of the direct meaning of the Canticle. We may recall that Theodore of Mopsuestia was condemned in the sixth century for proposing a literal interpretation, which practically everyone today would admit. Refusal to accept such an interpretation necessarily implied refusal to acknowledge sexual experience and to admit that if married love is in accord with God's will, sexual love must be too.

As is often the case, the common people knew better than the theologians. At least as early as the first Christian century, the Canticle was sung at banquets and wedding feasts, as we learn from the Mishnah, Josephus, and some Christian writers, and it has inspired more than one popular lyric in our own day.

"The most excellent song" of the one thousand and five

[8]I touched on this briefly in my *Celibacy, Ministry, Church* (New York: Herder and Herder, 1968), pp. 88-90.

traditionally ascribed to Solomon (1 Kings 4:32) is not really a song but a song-cycle and comes from a time long after Solomon had been dead and buried. We need not weary the reader with a detailed survey of all the attempts to explain the form and original purpose of this much-interpreted book. Most of these, after having enjoyed a run of popularity, have now been called into question and some are now of purely archaeological interest. Attempts to read it as a drama, after the fashion of the Greek *mimos*, were more ingenious than convincing since no progress towards a climax, even the climax of matrimony, can be observed. To suppose that it deals with a triangular tussle involving King Solomon, a country lass called to his harem, and her rustic lover is attractive but hardly less free of difficulties. In a recent issue of *The Saturday Review* (April 26, 1969), Kenneth Rexroth has suggested that it is a collection of dance lyrics for group marriage, lyrics which were sung as the young men and women danced in the cornfields and vineyards during the harvest festival corresponding to the Feast of Tents. This certainly comes nearer the mark, though the author seems to have forgotten the frequent references to springtime and the fact that the Canticle was used at Passover not Tents.

The most commonly heard view today is that it was put together as a song-cycle (whether for dancing or not) composed for a wedding celebration lasting seven days, as is still the case with Arabs in Syria and Palestine. Parallels between some of the lyrics and the Arab *wasf* or marriage-song have been discovered and some of them are quite impressive. It has also been noted that among Syro-Palestinian Arabs the first week after the wedding is called "the royal week," with the married couple playing the roles of king and queen. On the eve of the wedding, the bride performs a sword dance, which might explain the "camp dance" (a form of square dancing?) in 6:13. These and similar comparisons will certainly help us to appreciate these songs, though not everything will fit into the

wedding hypothesis, and there is certainly not enough material here to last for a week. It is, of course, possible that only a part of the original composition has survived. It may even be that some of the more frankly erotic lyrics have been screened out as less amenable to allegorical interpretation.

Some commentators have the idea that this song-cycle comes from the people and is therefore the product of a naive and rustic art. This is almost certainly false since where it falls short in artistic taste and perfection (as it often does, for a modern reader at least) the error is generally on the side of an excess of "conceit," an overabundance of far out images and metaphors and an overaddiction to such old stereotypes as the comparison of the beloved with a statue (Song 5:10-15). Its physical realism, while sometimes a little inaccessible to us, is generally direct and unembarrassed. The charms of the sun-burnt beauty from the country are spelled out in loving detail:

Behold, you are beautiful, my love,
    behold, you are beautiful!
Your eyes are doves
    behind your veil.
Your hair is like a flock of goats,
    moving down the slopes of Gilead.
Your teeth are like a flock of shorn ewes
    that have come up from the washing. . . .
Your lips are like a scarlet thread,
    and your mouth is lovely.
Your cheeks are like halves of a pomegranate
    behind your veil.
Your neck is like the tower of David
    built for an arsenal . . . .
Your two breasts are like two fawns,
    twins of a gazelle, that feed among the lilies. . . .
You are all fair, my love;
    there is no flaw in you (Song 4:1-7).

Her lover imagines he sees her naked, performing the sen-suous sword dance at the invitation of the chorus:

How graceful are your feet in sandals,
    O queenly maiden!
Your rounded thighs are like jewels,
    the work of a master hand.
Your navel is a rounded bowl
    that never lacks mixed wine.
Your belly is a heap of wheat,
    encircled with lilies.
Your two breasts are like two fawns,
    twins of a gazelle. . . (Song 7:1-3).

Everywhere there is erotic imagery, sometimes delicately
veiled in euphemism. She is a vineyard which she has not
looked after as she ought (1:6); she invites her lover to come to
the vineyard to see if the vines are budding and the blossoms
opening, promising him the gift of rarest fruits (7:12-13); she
is a palm tree and he vows to seize its clusters of grapes (7:
7-8); she offers him spiced wine, honey, and milk to drink
(8:1). And since chastity is also highly prized, she is a locked
garden and a sealed fountain (4:12). Here there is eroticism
which is sensuous and frank without a trace of vulgarity, bru-
tality, or salaciousness; a celebration of the gentleness, interiority, and even playfulness of awakening love between two
young people.

Everyone knows how easily sexual love becomes either ridic-
ulous or a bore when it is taken with absolute seriousness.
We cannot be certain that it was so intended by the writer,
but the chorus seems at times to provide a note of irony
which serves as a corrective to the intense preoccupation of
the two young lovers with one another. So, for example, we
may ask whether the address "loveliest of women" was really
wholly serious, especially since the girl, unlike the modern
beach beauty, had to apologize for her sunburnt skin. When
they ask:

Whither has your beloved gone,
    O fairest among women?

Whither has your beloved turned,
   that we may seek him with you? (Song 6:1).

there may well have been a note of sarcasm in their voices,
which was not lost on the young man, who later refers to them
as brambles surrounding his lily. Later on, the sarcasm turns
to exasperation as they answer this love-sick girl who continually pleads for their cooperation:

What is your beloved more than another beloved,
   O fairest among women?
What is your beloved more than another beloved,
   that you thus adjure us? (Song 5:9).

The answer is, of course, that the lovers, like all lovers, are
blind to any other beauty than that of each other—"I am my
beloved's and my beloved is mine!"

The motif of the search for the lost lover may, as has often
been suggested, owe something to the mythological motif of the
disappearing god. Echoes can also be heard here and there of
the divine marriage, the *hieros gamos,* consumated in the open
fields or the vineyards. This could hardly surprise us in view
of the allure which for centuries previously these rites had
exercised on the Hebrews. But this in itself would not justify
speaking of these lyrics as a veiled celebration of pagan mysteries. Hosea also uses language familiar in the fertility cult; in
fact, this idiom must have been almost inescapable when speaking at length of human love and its celebration. The search
passages in the songs speak at the most obvious level of the
sexual fantasies of a young girl just past puberty who keenly
anticipates the joys of sexual love. In imagination she is already
in her lover's arms—"his left arm is under my head, his right
embraces me." She imagines he is looking in through the win-
dow at her as she lies sleepless on her bed. So vivid does the
image become that in her fantasy she gets up and wanders
through the deserted city streets looking for him:

Upon my bed by night
   I sought him whom my soul loves;
I sought him, but found him not;
   I called him, but he gave no answer.
"I will rise now and go about the city,
   in the streets and in the squares;
I will seek him whom my soul loves."
   I sought him, but found him not (Song 3:1-2).

As often happens in dream or daydream, the object of her search appears, seems to be within her grasp, and then fades from sight. In one sequence the youth comes naked to her door at night, she trembles to the core of her being, but no sooner does she get to the door and open it but he vanishes into the night air. In her fantasy she goes after him, is arrested by the city police as a prostitute, beaten, and then released to find her way home. All she can do as she comes back to herself is turn to the chorus and ask them to tell her lover that she is sick with love (5:8).

These imaginings of a love-sick girl in the season when "the flowers appear on the earth and the time of singing has come" hardly seem to amount to much in terms of religious or theological significance. Yet, the remarkable thing is that they are *there,* embarrassingly, awkwardly there among the laws, the priestly Torah and the prophetic oracles of doom. These songs, distilled from the life of a people scored by the lash of a fierce and urgent God, speak of the holiness of union between man and woman and testify that wherever love—even adolescent love—is born, there is potentiality for something hot as flame, tenacious as hell, strong as death. This is, in fact, what the collector of the songs or a later editor states toward the end:

Love is strong as death,
Jealousy is cruel as the grave.
Its flashes are flashes of fire,
a most vehement flame.

Many waters cannot quench love,
neither can floods drown it.

—to which has been added a last reflection: "If a man offered for love all the wealth of his house, it would be utterly scorned" (Song 8:6-7).

The human love and sexual joy which this nameless young couple celebrate together present us with an invitation and a challenge. At the risk of exaggerating, we could say that the traditional Christian ideal has been much closer to Jerome's Tobit and Sarah, who can consummate their union only after three days of exorcizing the demon of lust by common prayer. Outside of this view of a happy Christian marriage, there are those other partners, Tristan and Iseult, Romeo and Juliet, and a hundred others whose desire for each other ends not in physical union but in death—thus illustrating the "Christian" principle that love cannot be perfected in the body. It seems that only when we affirm the reality of bodily love can we assent to the Jewish and Christian tradition which sees in it the reflection of "the great mystery" by which God loves his people and draws near to them. For if it is only an illusion, an infatuation, a temptation, or a snare, there is nothing to reflect and nothing to celebrate.

INDEX

Adam, 26, 27
adam (mankind), 27
agape, 8, 30, 39
Agape and Eros, 8, 8f.
ahavah (love), 8, 9, 39
akitu (New Year festival), 20, 21, 34
Amis, Kingsley, 83, 84
Amos, 55, 105
Anath, 23, 25
Ancient Near Eastern Texts Relating to the Old Testament, 109f.
androgyny, 23, 28-30
Anthony, St., 34
Antigone, 28
Aphrodite, 16, 23
Apsu, 21, 34
Aqhat, 23
Aquinas, Thomas, 8, 9
argumentum ad hominem, 60, 61
Aristophanes, 7, 19
Aristotle, 18
Asherah, 24, 25
Asmodeus, 34
Augustine, St., 9, 65, 108, 115

Baal, 23, 25
Bailey, D. Sherwin, 46f., 72
Bergson, Henri, 18
Black, M., 59f.
The Body: A Study in Pauline Theology, 78f.
Bonhoeffer, Dietrich, 66, 66f., 79f.

Cain, 28
Camus, Albert, 64, 110
Canticle of Canticles, 115-121
castration and circumcision, relationship between, 33, 70, 71

celebration, 102-121;
    acknowledge death to enjoy life 109-113;
    to dance, 102-105, 107;
    to laugh, 103, 107;
    to make love, 102-104, 108, 115-121
celibacy, 30, 89-91;
    clerical, 47, 48;
    of Yahweh, 24-41
Celibacy, Ministry, Church, 115f.
Ceres, 16
chaos, 18, 21, 22, 27, 34
Christ of Kazantzakis, 96-101
Christian Tradition, *See* Tradition
church-Christianity, 17
Comfort, Alex, 19, 40f., 102
Commandments, *See* decalogue
concupiscence, 9, 10
covenant,
    annulment of, 40;
    divine, 37, 38;
    -law relationship, 12, 37, 51, 53, 55, 56, 65;
    of friendship, 38;
    of marriage, 38, 48
Cox, Harvey, 16, 16f.
Creation and Fall, Temptation, 66f.
culture-Christianity, 16

Daedalus, Stephen, 6, 45
David, 26, 28, 32, 34, 104;
    and Bathsheba, 53, 113;
    and Jonathan, 38
de Beauvoir, Simone, 72, 72f.
decalogue, 42, 46, 47, 49, 50, 51, 53, 55, 59, 68
demythologizing of sexuality, 21, 25, 33, 40, 82
Deuteronomy, 47, 51-53

123

Dionysus, 21, 104, 110
divorce laws, 40, 47, 48, 57, 89, 90
Donne, John, 78
Douglas, Lloyd, 94
Driver, Tom F., 81, 81f., 82, 83, 85-88, 94, 95
dromenon, 20
Duncan, Ronald, 94

Ebeling, Gerhard, 18f.
El, 23, 24, 27;
    Yahweh-El, 24
Eliade, M., 22f., 23f., 28f.
Empedocles, 7
Enuma Elish, 107
eros, 3-15;
    and fun, 102, 118;
    as dark force or *hubris*, 7, 28;
    "crucifixion" of, 10, 11;
    humanizing of, 17, 19, 33-35, 40, 115-121;
    meaning of, 6, 7;
    relationship with concupiscence, 9, 10;
    relationship with Tradition, 3-7;
    role in society, 35;
    separation of "love" and "sex," 14, 17
Ethics, 79f.
eunuchs, three classes of, 89-92
The Extasie, 78
Ezekiel, 25, 35, 36, 108

familial relationships, 35-37, 92, 108
father, as son's rival, 31-33, 70, 71
Fletcher, Joseph, 56, 56f.
Freedman, D. N., 30f.
freedom, 63-80;
    and law, 41, 50, 59, 60, 62, 63, 68-72;
    and responsibility, 64, 66, 67, 74-80;
    economic, 63;
    no necessity to "prove" self, 95;
    of individual Christian, 73, 74;
    political, 63;
    relationship between two persons, 66, 74, 80;
    sexual, 62-66, 72, 75-80, 108
Freud, Sigmund, 10, 14, 31-33, 44, 49, 53, 54, 70, 113
Fromm, Eric, 45, 45f.

Genesis, 21, 23f., 25-27, 30, 64, 65, 87, 107
Gide, André, 64
Gilgamesh, 22, 23
Gnostic heresy, *See* heresies
gods and goddesses,
    as sexual partners, 18, 23, 24, 28;
    individual goddesses: Anath, 23, 25; Aphrodite, 16, 23; Asherah, 24, 25; Ishtar, 23, 29; Kali, 22; Tiamat, 21, 27, 34;
    individual gods: Apsu, 21, 34; Baal, 23, 25; El, 23, 24, 27; Osiris, 23
Goethe, Johann, 10
Gordis, Robert, 14, 14f., 72
Gordon, C. H., 23f.
Gospel of Thomas, 30, 87
Gould, Thomas, 7f.
The Graduate, 43
Graf-Wellhausen hypothesis, 49
Grant, R. M., 30f.
The Greek Passion, 6, 100

Hammurabi, 50, 51
Harris poll, 4
Hefner, Hugh, 19
heresies, 9;
    Gnostics, 10, 30, 75, 82, 86-88, 93;
    Manicheans, 10, 86, 87;
    prophets as "heretics," 12
hermaphrodite, 7, 24
Hermas, 58
Heschel, Abraham J., 56, 56f., 106, 106f.
hesed, 9, 38, 39
Hesnard, Dr., 45, 45f., 54
hieros gamos, 119
homosexuality, 38, 45, 46, 84
Homosexuality and the Western Christian Tradition, 46
Hosea, 25, 35, 37-40, 48, 55, 115, 119
hubris, 7, 28
Humanae Vitae, 19, 42

humanization of sexuality, 17, 19, 33-35, 40, 115-121
Huxley, Aldous, 28

Ignatius of Antioch, 6, 7, 10
Ikhnaton, 32
Ireland, and sexuality, 5, 6
Isaksson, Abel, 91f.
Ishtar, 23, 29
Isis, 16, 23

Jacob, E., 34f.
Jeremiah, 12, 25, 38, 55, 106
Jerome, 46-48, 114, 121
Jesus Christ, 12, 30, 52, 56-62, 69-71, 73, 76-78, 81-101, 112;
    humanity of, 81-83, 84-86, 94-96;
    untouched by sexual desire, 81-87, 93, 95
Job, Book of, 13, 32, 33, 109
Joyce, James, 5, 6
Judas, 94
Judeo-Christian Tradition, See Tradition
Jung, Carl, 19
Justinian, 46

Kali, 22
Kazantzakis, Helen, 101f.
Kazantzakis, Nikos, 6, 13, 14, 14f., 32, 33, 33f., 84, 84f., 95, 96, 96f., 97, 97f., 98, 98f., 99, 99f., 100, 103f.
Kazantzakis, Nikos: A Biography Based on His Letters, 101f.
Kierkegaard, Sören, 10
Kinsey, Alfred, 75
Krafft-Ebing, Baron Richard von, 75

Lady Chatterley's lover, 6
The Last Temptation of Christ, 6, 96, 96f., 97f., 101
law, 41-62;
    and love, 56, 58, 59, 61, 62;
    association with community, 50-52, 69;
    capacity to accept others, 61, 62, 69;
    creative realism, 59, 60, 94;
    history and functions, 40, 49-55, 70;
    observance as way of life, 54, 55, 59, 61;
    refusal to judge others, 60;
    relationship with freedom, 41, 50, 59, 60, 62, 63, 68-72
The Laws in the Pentateuch and Other Essays, 50f.
Lawrence, D. H., 11, 17, 19, 83, 94, 100
legalism, 3, 48, 55, 57, 59, 69, 107
love, See also concupiscence, eros, sexuality;
    agape, 8, 30, 39;
    ahavah, 8, 9, 39;
    and "sex," 14, 17;
    aquisitive, 8;
    benevolent, 8;
    Christian, 3, 8;
    Christ's attitude toward, 59-62;
    concupiscent, 8, 9;
    divine, 9, 39;
    erotic, 11, 30, 118;
    hesed (steadfast), 9, 38, 39;
    human, 9, 39, 87, 115-121;
    of the world, 10;
    passionate, 10;
    self-transcending and immolating, 9;
    sexual, 4, 7-9, 119;
    spontaneous, 8

McLuhan, Marshall, 5
Mailer, Norman, 19
"The Man Who Died," 83
the Man and the Woman, 25-27, 64, 65
man-woman relationship, 3, 7, 37-40, 57, 102, 113, 114
Manichean heresy, See heresies
Marriage and Ministry in the New Temple, 91f.
Marty, M. E., 81f., 83f., 86f., 95f.
Mary, 30, 77, 82
masturbation, 47
Merleau-Ponty, quotation from, 18
Miller, Henry, 19
Mirgeler, Albert, 6f.
Montefiore, Canon Hugh, 83
Moralité sans Peché, 45, 45f.
Moses, 32, 35, 36, 49, 51
Moses and Monotheism, 31

Mowinckel, Sigmund, 20, 20f.
Mozart, Wolfgang, 10
Mutations of Western Christianity,
6f.
mystics, 9, 12
mythology, 16-41, 63, 67, 119
mythos, 20

Nero, 10
New Testament, *See* Scripture
New Theology No. 3, 81f., 83f.,
86f., 95f.
Nietzsche, Friedrich, 21, 64, 96,
105
Noth, M., 50f.
Nygren, Anders, 8, 8f.

O'Brien, Edna, 5
O'Casey, Sean, 5
Old Testament, *See* Scripture
Old Testament Theology, 12f.
Onan, 47
original sin, 26, 44, 49
orgy, 20-22, 33, 66, 67
Osiris, 23

Packard, Vance, 75
Patterns in Comparative Religion,
22f., 23f., 28f.
Paul, St., 7, 11, 15, 55, 68-80, 85,
92
Peake's Commentary on the Bible,
59f.
Peerman, D. G., 81f., 83f., 86f.,
95f.
Philo, 46
Plato, 7, 8, 18, 19, 24, 29, 31,
105-107
Plato: The Man and His Work, 7f.
Platonic Love, 7f.
Playboy of the Western World, 5
Pritchard, James B., 109f.
prophets, 12, 13, 20, 25, 29, 36,
49, 52, 54-56, 61, 67, 105-107,
113, 115, 120
The Prophets, 56f.
Proverbs, Book of, 108, 113, 114
Proverbs and Ecclesiastes, 113f.
Psalms, 32
Psalmenstudien, 20f.
Psychoanalyse et Religion, 45, 45f.

Psychoanalysis and Religion, 45,
45f.
"psychodelic generation," 4

Qoheleth, 109-112
Qumran community, 48, 73, 90, 91,
93

"radial energy," 7
Ras Shamra tablets, 23, 24
"Re-judaizing Christianity," 14f.
Report to Greco, 14f., 33f., 84,
84f., 97f., 98f., 99, 103, 103f.
Republic, 19
Rexroth, Kenneth, 116
Ricoeur, Paul, 54, 55, 55f., 61
Rilke, R. M., 84, 84f.
Robinson, J. A. T., 78f.
"the rotted past," 44
Rowley, H. H., 59f.

Sartre, Jean-Paul, 64
Satan, 34, 87, 95
Sauty, Roger, 45, 45f.
Sayers, Dorothy L., 94
Scott, R. B. Y., 113f.
Scripture, *See also* Tradition;
Christian (New Testament), 6,
8, 31, 52, 57-62, 71, 81-95,
110;
Jewish (Old Testament), 6, 8,
12, 13, 17, 20, 21, 24, 26-28,
32, 39, 40, 45-47, 49, 50, 52,
64, 65, 90, 104-121
The Second Sex, 72f.
The Secret Sayings of Jesus, 30f.
The Secular City, 16f.
Selected Letters of R. M. Rilke,
84f.
Seth, 27
Sex in Society, 40f.
"sex in the head," 17
sexual
conduct, 31, 42, 48, 49, 51, 52,
73;
mysticism, 19, 28-30, 38;
promiscuity, 26, 75, 79;
relations, 73, 75, 76, 91-93;
symbols, 16, 21
taboos, 47, 71, 107
sexuality, *See also* celebration,
eros, concupiscence, love;

and dancing, 5, 102-105;
and fun, 102;
and guilt, 5, 6, 17, 44, 45, 47, 54, 71;
churches' attitude toward, 5, 6, 16, 42-62, 72-95, 102-104;
inherently evil, 49, 86, 87
Sexuality and Jesus, 81, 81f.
Shakespeare, William, 103, 114
Shelley, Percy, 24
Situation Ethics, 56f.
situationists, 55, 56
A Sketchbook of Biblical Theology, 26f.
Snyder, Ross, 44f.
Sodom, 114;
and Gomorrah, 46
Solomon, 26, 34, 113, 115, 116
The Song of Songs, 115-121
Speiser, E. A., 23f.
Supplement to Vetus Testamentum, 26f.
symbols, 19, 35, 36;
Christian (traditional), 4, 15, 16, 64, 67;
sexual, 16,21
Symposium, 7, 19, 105
Synge, John, 5

Talmud, 49, 49f.
Taylor, A. E., 7f.
tehom, 21, 27
Teilhard de Chardin, 7
Thammuz, 23
Theology of the Old Testament, 34f.
theology of sexuality, 17
Tiamat, 21, 27, 34
Tillich, Paul, 9, 10, 10f., 19
Timaeus, 19

Tobit, 114
Tobit, 34, 121
Torah, 58, 59, 65, 68, 87, 120
Totem and Taboo, 31
Tradition, *See also* Scripture;
and freedom, 67;
and the Gospels, 81-95;
application to present culture, 4, 12, 16, 17, 44;
challenge of today, 13, 15;
defined, 12;
relationship with celebration, or *eros,* 3, 4, 41-62, 102-104, 115-121;
relationship with church authority, 11, 12, 42-62;
relationship with myths, 24;
sexual prohibitions, 53
transvestism, 28, 29

Ugaritic Literature, 23f.

von Rad, Gerhard, 12, 12f., 42f.

The Wisdom of Solomon, 110
wisdom teachers, 12, 13, 21, 26, 27, 65, 108-110, 113, 114
Word and Faith, 18f.
"word-event," 18, 18f.
Wordsworth, William, 24

Yahweh, 14, 51, 97;
Yahweh-El, 24;
without spouse or offspring, 24-41
Yeats, William B., 5

zanah, 25
Zeus, 27
Zorba, 103
Zorba the Greek, 110